America's FUNNY BUT TRUE History 1800-1850 WESTWARD, HA-HA!

by **Elizabeth Levy**

Illustrated by **Daniel McFeeley**

with Additional Material by **J. R. Havlan**

SCHOLASTIC INC.
New York   Toronto   London   Auckland   Sydney
Mexico City   New Delhi   Hong Kong   Buenos Aires

To Robie Harris
—E. L.

Scholastic gratefully acknowledges the original inspiration of Terry Deary's *Horrible Histories* series, published by Scholastic Publications Ltd., London, U.K.

ISBN 0-590-12257-6
Text copyright © 2003 by Elizabeth Levy

Illustrations copyright © 2003 by Scholastic Inc.
All rights reserved. Published by Scholastic Inc.

SCHOLASTIC and associated logos are trademarks and/or registered trademarks of Scholastic Inc.
12 11 10 9 8 7 6 5 4 3 2   3 4 5 6 7 8/0   40

Printed in the U.S.A.
First printing, December 2003

www.ElizabethLevy.com

Contents

Funny But True

History is usually a random, messy affair. . . .
Mark Twain, *A Horse's Tail*

The one who tells the stories rules the world.
Hopi saying

Sometimes the funniest things are true. Meriwether Lewis and William Clark wrote about their farts. Sam Houston of Texas was the first man to wear beads in Congress. *America's Funny But True History* is about just this kind of real, factual, *funny* history.

There's a saying that if you don't know your own history, you are condemned to repeat it. I say that if we can't laugh at ourselves, we're in even worse trouble. Human beings do odd, strange things and no one people has a monopoly on making mistakes. History is all about real lives and real people — and these same people often loved to tell a joke. If you can share a joke, it's hard to hate.

There are facts and jokes in *Westward, Ha-ha!* that will make you laugh out loud, some that will make you grin and groan, and others that will make you squirm. While you're laughing, remember, the information in this book is true, at least as far as anybody knows.

My best teachers were always the ones who could laugh. One wonderful teacher, my rabbi, once told me that nobody can ever know the whole truth, but that it's worth holding on to those little slivers of truth that we do find. It's hard to find the truth in history. There is always new historical information being discovered that gives us new ways of looking at history. Ideas about what really happened in the past change as often as most people change their underwear!

Introduction

The United States was barely a teenager in 1800. Its western border ended east of the Mississippi River, and its population was only a little more than five million. If you were one of those five million or so people, the odds were one in five that you were a slave. Chances were two to three that you lived within 50 miles of

Yo, yo, yo! Moms! All my peeps sport dis weave.

I have no idea what you just said, but get right back in this house and change those clothes!

Uncle Sam as a Kid

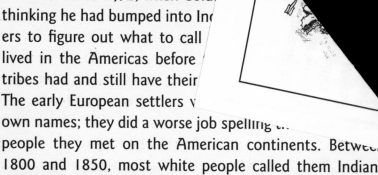

What's in a [

Ever since 1492, when Colum
thinking he had bumped into Inc
ers to figure out what to call
lived in the Americas before
tribes had and still have their
The early European settlers v
own names; they did a worse job spelling ...
people they met on the American continents. Betwee..
1800 and 1850, most white people called them Indians
(when they weren't calling them nastier names). In this
book, I've used the names of the tribes, but if the tribal
name is unknown, I've used the words *tribes* or *Native
Americans*.

the Atlantic Ocean. West of the Mississippi lay
more than two million square miles of territory cut
through by the Rocky Mountains. This land did *not*
belong to the United States.

Westward, Ha-ha! covers the period from 1800
to 1850, when Spaniards, Mexicans, Americans,
Pueblo, Navajo, Ute, Lakota, Cheyenne, Apache,
and many other tribes galloped, traded, traveled by
wagons, and fought up and down the valleys,
mountains, and riverbanks of the West. In 1803,
Thomas Jefferson doubled the size of the United
States with the Louisiana Purchase. By 1850,
through war, purchase, and treaties, the United
States had grown by 2,103,935 square miles.

Meet the Wild and Not So Wild Bunch

Throughout this book you'll meet a lot of real-life characters. A lot of them like Jim Bowie, Antonio López de Santa Anna, Davy Crockett, Lola Montez, and Mike Fink were really wild. Others like Sacajawea, Narcissa Whitman, Levi Strauss, and Kit Carson weren't so wild. But all of them went where it was wild and where it took a lot of grit to go. I'm hoping they won't mind being bunched together. I'd like to think that they'd be a little flattered. So, get ready to meet some pretty amazing characters whenever you see the Wild Bunch and The Not So Wild Bunch icon.

By 1800, very few Native Americans in the West were living the way their ancestors had. The horse, brought over by the Spanish in the 1500s, changed the way tribes hunted and fought.

By the 19th century, the tribes of the West had welcomed another European import into their culture: guns. Tribes that became really good at fighting with horses and guns began to rule the West.

When American citizens took off in their covered wagons for what is now California, Oregon, and Texas, some of them really did shout, "Westward, ho!" Most of those heading west didn't have a good idea what they were getting into. Still, they knew they were going on an adventure. I'm going to tell you the funny but true parts of this adventure. (And because it's history there are lots of not-so-funny parts.) So sit back, and welcome to *Westward, Ha-ha!*

Elizabeth Levy

Hi, everybody!

Remember me? I assume you do, since I'm sure you read the first five books in America's Funny But True History series, but just in case, allow me to re-re-re-re-reintroduce myself. I'm the inimitable Mel Roach. That's right, "inimitable." It's a fancy word that means "there's nobody like me." I learned it from a piece of paper some mean old man rolled up and tried to squash me with. But don't worry! It's not that easy to get rid of me. Go ahead. You give it a try. First, remember what page you're on; then slam the book shut real hard right on my face; then open it back up to this page. Go ahead. Slam it real hard right on the old kisser. . . . See? You can't get rid of me. I'm like the pimple that pops up on your big brother or sister's face the night before the school dance. I'm not going anywhere! So why don't you and I just settle in and see what Liz, that nice lady who wrote this book, has to say about how America went from being a skinny little kid to a big, strong, full-grown country. I think it had something to do with drinking plenty of milk and eating lots of vegetables . . . but, then again, I've been wrong before.

Chapter 1
Look What $15,000,000 Got US!

In January of 1800, except for Oregon (claimed by the British and the United States), if you lived in the more than two million square miles that we call the West, you were ruled by Spain. At least that's what Spain liked to think. For more than 300 years, Spain had tried to govern this huge area from the distant capitals of Mexico City, Mexico, and Madrid, Spain. The problem was that not many Spaniards wanted to leave the comfort of

TIME LINE

1769 to 1823
Spanish missions in
California

1803
Louisiana
Purchase

1804
Meriwether Lewis,
William Clark, and
their Corps of
Discovery start
out

Spain or the gold and glamour of Mexico City to go out into the wilderness.

California: Mission Impossible

Starting in 1769, the Spanish rulers in Mexico City sent groups of Spanish priests into what is now California. The priests' mission (which they accepted) was to convert the tribes they met to Catholicism. The priests traveled with a small group of soldiers and wherever they could, they forced Native Americans to build "missions" up and down the California coast.

From 1769 to 1823, Spanish priests and soldiers and California natives built 21 missions under the leadership of Father Junípero Serra. Each mission was part fort, part farm, and part church. The missions were like little islands of Spanish culture, government, and religion in a huge sea of Native American–dominated lands. At the time, there were between 200,000 and 300,000 non-Spanish-speaking people living in California. They were the Chumash, the Pomo, the Modoc, and many other tribes.

1805
With Sacajawea's help, Lewis and Clark reach the Pacific Ocean

1809
Lewis commits suicide (or does he?)

1814
Lewis and Clark's journals published. Read all about it!

California had rich farmland, a warm climate, and rivers full of fish. The Native Americans in California were living quite well without the Europeans. The Spaniards said they had come to save the Native Americans, but in the Spanish missions, the natives were forced to do all the work and to live almost as slaves.

Spain Makes a Secret Deal

On October 1, 1800, Spain had decided a lot of its land north of present-day Mexico was more trouble than it was worth. Spain chose to hold on to what it thought were the good parts — California,

Father Junípero Serra and How the San Diego Padres Got Their Name

When Father Serra became a priest, he asked to be called Junípero, after a jester, or jokester, who had lived with Saint Francis of Assisi.

"Class clown" is not the first thing you would think of if you met Father Junípero Serra. He believed that suffering made him pure. He was painfully thin, and it must have hurt his butt to ride a mule for hundreds of miles through the roadless California territory.

Father Serra traveled up and down the California coast, naming places for Christian saints, for example: Santa Barbara, San Francisco, San Juan Capistrano, and San Luis Obispo. Serra's first mission was built in San Diego, and that is how the San Diego Padres baseball team got their name. *Padre* is the Spanish word for father or priest.

California Missions. You can follow **El Camino Real** (also known as King's Highway) along the California coast from San Diego to San Francisco and find the remains of the 21 Spanish missions. Many of the old missions have been made into historical sites and many still have active churches. Along the way you'll also see some of the most beautiful scenery in the world.

Texas, and the territory of New Mexico — but to secretly sell all the rest to France. France had a new dictator, Napoleon Bonaparte. Napoleon just loved the idea of an empire. The problem was his eyes were bigger than his stomach. Napoleon tried to swallow all of Europe, including Russia, and failed. He also tried to swallow a lot of pastries.

Think of him whenever you eat a Napoleon pastry. It's supposed to be named for him. According to a Danish legend (think Danish pastries), a Danish chef made it for Emperor Napoleon and the king of Denmark, and the chocolate squiggles on top are supposed to look like the letter N.

By 1803, Napoleon began having second thoughts about starting a huge empire in the New World. France couldn't even hold on to the tiny island of Haiti. The slaves in Haiti revolted against France and won their independence in a brutal war. Napoleon needed money to fight his wars in Europe. Fortunately for him, the United States had a new president who had big dreams and was interested in making a purchase.

Anybody Seen a Woolly Mammoth or a Mastodon?

In 1801, the first complete skeleton of a mastodon was found near Newburgh, New York. The mastodon was a giant elephantlike creature that once roamed North America alongside the woolly mammoth. The skeleton was nicknamed the American Monster, and people wondered if such creatures still existed.

No one wanted to see a live mastodon more than Thomas Jefferson. He figured that if this creature lived anywhere, it would be in the unexplored (by white people, that is) land west of the Mississippi River. The West fascinated Jefferson and he had more books in his library on the West than could be found anywhere else in the world.

Jefferson was nearly 58 years old when he became the third president of the United States in 1801. One of the first things Jefferson did was convince Congress to give him secret authorization to send a small "Corps of Discovery" on an exploration west. The Corps was to find out if there was a river that cut through the West. Ever since Christopher Columbus's time, Europeans had been trying to find a waterway from the Atlantic to the Pacific oceans. The Corps was also supposed to look for prehistoric creatures and anything else they could find.

Thomas "Shop Till You Drop" Jefferson

At the time of the secret authorization, Jefferson thought the western lands belonged to Spain. Now, if Spain had sent its explorers through the United States, you can bet that President Jefferson would have been hopping mad. But Jefferson figured a few men in a huge territory wouldn't cause too much of a fuss.

In 1803, before his Corps of Discovery could take off, President Jefferson tried to buy the port of New Orleans from Napoleon. Napoleon played a

game of Let's Make a Deal! He offered to sell the United States *all* the land France had just bought from Spain. The deal was for more than 827,192 square miles. It was called the Louisiana Purchase for all the French kings named Louis (the last one, Louis XVI, lost his head in the French Revolution). Today, the Louisiana Purchase comprises the states of Louisiana, Arkansas, Oklahoma, Missouri, Kansas, Nebraska, Iowa, Minnesota, South Dakota, North Dakota, most of Wyoming and Montana, eastern Colorado, and tiny bits of New Mexico and Texas.

Napoleon was willing to sell the Louisiana Purchase for $15,000,000, or just under three cents an acre. But $15,000,000 was a lot of money for a new little country. If you piled 15 million dollar bills on top of each other, the stack would reach three miles high. Still, President Jefferson made the deal, which nearly bankrupted the United States treasury.

Jefferson was desperate to find out what he had bought. Even before the purchase, he had picked his young secretary, Meriwether Lewis, to lead the Corps of Discovery. Lewis asked an old friend, William Clark, to be his cocaptain. Now their trip was even more important. The whole country was anxious to find out what was in the Louisiana Purchase. It was like buying a big new house without ever seeing it. Jefferson told Lewis and Clark to hurry up and get on their way. Only now their orders were different. He didn't just want them to explore. He wanted them to tell all the native tribes

Meriwether Lewis (1774–1809) and William Clark (1770–1838)

Meriwether Lewis was born in Virginia. When he was just 17 years old, Thomas Jefferson invited him to live in the president's house and be his secretary. Like Jefferson, Lewis loved to learn. Lewis was extremely bright, but he could be moody and sometimes drank too much.

William Clark was born into a Virginia plantation family in 1770. When Clark was 14, his family moved to a new plantation in Kentucky. Clark would spend the rest of his life on what was then America's frontier. Everybody liked him; he was smart but didn't get upset when things went wrong. Lewis and Clark were so different that you might think they would hate each other. Clark was older than Lewis, and he sometimes resented the fact that Lewis had been asked to lead the Corps first. But basically, the two men turned out to be the best of friends. Their names will be forever linked in history as the leaders of the first United States citizens to go overland to the Pacific Ocean.

they met the news: They were now part of the United States.

Lewis and Clark Take Off

On May 14, 1804, Lewis and Clark and 31 men, mostly young bachelors, pushed off from St. Louis going upstream on the Missouri River. At least three of the men were sons of white fathers and Native American mothers. These men would serve as translators when they met Native American tribes. There was one black man in the Corps, York, who was William Clark's slave from the time he was a child. York and Clark had grown up together.

Lewis kept a detailed journal, and he told every man on the trip to keep one, too. Both Lewis and Clark were two of the worst spellers who ever lived, even by the standards of their day.

On May 14, 1804, "under a jentle brease" (you figure it out), the Corps of Discovery pushed out into the Missouri River. The current pushed them right back. The mast of their big boat snapped. The men had to wade along the muddy banks of the Missouri and pull the boat against the current with ropes. As they traveled upriver, through territory that is now Missouri and Iowa, Clark, who was the better boatman, took charge of the boats. Lewis walked along the banks with his big Newfoundland dog, Seaman.

On August 5, just a few months into their trip, Sergeant Charles Floyd became very sick. On

Thunderbolts

Historians think that Sergeant Charles Floyd had a burst appendix and nothing could have saved him. But Lewis tried. Before the trip, President Jefferson had sent Lewis to study medicine with the leading doctor of the day, Dr. Benjamin Rush of Philadelphia. Dr. Rush gave Lewis 600 pills nicknamed "thunderbolts."

"These will scour a man out like a chimney swept's brush. . . . You'll have your men sprouting at both ends," Dr. Rush told Lewis. "I would recommend not having them in the canoe with you when you physick 'em."

Lewis gave Floyd a thunderbolt — it didn't work.

August 20, near what is now Sioux City, Iowa, on a bluff overlooking the river, the sergeant died. His last words to Lewis were "I'm going away." It was the first death on the trip. Most of the men thought there would be many others.

During the first part of the trip, the Corps of Discovery traveled through what we now call the Great Plains, one of the largest grasslands in the world. The grass grew as tall as a horse's belly. Lewis and Clark thought the land would never be good for farming. Eventually, these prairies of modern-day Nebraska and Kansas would be called the "breadbasket" of the United States because so much wheat is grown there.

In the 1800s, most white Americans didn't believe that anything good could grow in a land that didn't have trees. The prairies just went on and on. Buffalo herds stretched across the horizon as deep and plentiful as chickens on a farm, and the rivers were full of beavers.

Lewis kept looking for Native Americans so he could tell them they were now part of the United States. But Lewis and Clark didn't know that almost all of the tribes in the Great Plains were out hunting buffalo. For nearly two months the Corps didn't see any other people. But they ran into plenty of other creatures.

Children, Meet Your New Father (Why Didn't He Bring Better Presents?)

Finally, near what is now Omaha, Nebraska, Lewis and Clark ran into a small group of people from the Oto and Missouri tribes. Lewis gave a speech that his guides translated. "Children, we of the seventeen nations [there were now seventeen states] have a new great father in Washington who welcomes you. Children, follow his council and you won't have anything to fear."

"Okay," said most of the chiefs of the tribes as they smoked pipes together. Most of the tribes were used to white people telling them that they came in peace. Luckily for the tribes, so far, very few white people had tried to live among them. Most of the tribes *did* want to trade. But Lewis and Clark had

What's Got Two Wings and Is Very Troublesome?

"Musquitters," as William Clark called them.

The mosquitoes were so bad that the dog, Seaman, howled at night because of them. In the men's journals, mosquitoes are described as "troublesome, very troublesome, uncommonly troublesome, exceedingly, immensely numerous and troublesome." In short, everybody hated the bugs. The mosquitoes were so thick that the men coated themselves in bear grease for protection.

very little to offer — a little tobacco, some medals with Jefferson's picture on one side and two hands clasped in peace on the other. Most chiefs were not too pleased with these meager presents. They were much more interested in guns, but Lewis and Clark would not trade their guns.

"If We Eat, You Will Eat"

After six months, Lewis and Clark arrived at the Mandan villages north of what is now Bismarck, North Dakota. The Mandans were famous farmers and traders. Cree, Shoshones, Crows, Spaniards, Frenchmen, and Englishmen all came to the Mandan villages to trade. The Mandan invited Lewis and Clark to build a fort across the river from where they lived. The Mandan town had a population of about 4,500. "If we eat, you will eat, and if we starve, you will starve also," the Mandan chief told them. Living with the Mandan was a young Shoshone woman called Sacajawea. Her image would end up on a U.S. gold coin in the 21st century.

Off into the Unknown

On April 7, with her eight-week-old baby strapped to her back, Sacajawea took off with the Corps of Discovery, the only woman among the 30-odd men headed for the Pacific. Lewis and Clark had sent a few men back to Washington with letters and specimens for Jefferson, including a live prairie dog.

Sacajawea (1786?–1812)

Sacajawea, a Shoshone, grew up high up in the Rocky Mountains in Wyoming. Her tribe didn't come in much contact with white people. When she was probably 10 or 11 years old, a rival tribe kidnapped her and then sold her in a gambling game to a French-Canadian fur trader, Toussaint Charbonneau. Charbonneau had brought Sacajawea to the Mandan village. Now she was having his baby, and she was probably about 20 years old, or even younger.

Lewis and Clark decided to take Charbonneau, Sacajawea, and her infant son, Jean-Baptiste, with them, so that Charbonneau could act as an interpreter. The fact that Sacajawea was a Shoshone sealed the deal. Lewis and Clark knew they would need the help of the Shoshones to trade for horses to get across the Rockies.

Both Meriwether Lewis and especially William Clark became very fond of Sacajawea, nicknaming her Janey. They called her son Pomp. Clark particularly was taken with the baby, saying he was a "butifull promising Child."

Sacajawea vs. Her Husband: No Contest

In the spring, after leaving the Mandan and North Dakota, the Corps of Discovery were soon dragging their useless canoes through the high plains of Montana. They desperately needed horses because Clark was sick with a high fever and had an ankle wound. His feet were so blistered he could hardly walk. Tempers were short. Supplies were running short, too. If the Corps were trapped in the Rockies in the winter snow, they would die.

Very quickly, Lewis and Clark figured out that Sacajawea's husband, Charbonneau, was the kind of cranky klutz who causes accidents and always blames someone else, but they kept him around because of Sacajawea. The Corps might never have made it if it hadn't been for her. First of all, when many of the Native Americans saw that the white men were traveling with a Shoshone woman and a baby, they decided the Corps wasn't a war party.

Journeys of a Prairie Dog

As they moved through the Great Plains, Lewis and Clark kept coming upon vast cities of little creatures, each poking their heads up out of their tunnels. None of the Corps had ever seen a prairie dog before. Lewis wrote in his journal, ". . . we got to have one of them." Everybody in the Corps got into the act of trying to catch a prairie dog. They shoved ramrods down their holes and poured water into their tunnels. Lewis wrote that the little creatures seemed to be laughing at them. The prairie dogs would "poke their heads up and stand erect and slip away from us." Finally, they caught one and put it in a cage. That little prairie dog ended up alive at the White House. Thomas Jefferson was so interested in the animal that he sent the prairie dog to scientists in Philadelphia. The animal lived out the rest of its days in Independence Hall, where 30 years earlier, the Declaration of Independence had been publicly read.

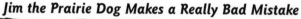

Jim the Prairie Dog Makes a Really Bad Mistake

Then, according to the men's journals, Sacajawea saved the day more than once. For example, when an expedition boat almost tipped over, she kept her baby in her arms, but somehow managed to save Lewis's compass and, most important of all for history buffs, his journals. Sacajawea also helped the group find food, such as wild artichokes, that had been stored by mice. She taught Lewis and Clark to leave a little grain behind as a thank-you for the mice. On the other hand, she got them lost more than once and was really not a much better guide than her husband.

A Hollywood Happy Ending

Sometimes things happen in history that truly sound like a Hollywood screenwriter made it up. That's what happened to Sacajawea. In the midst of thousands of square miles of wilderness, Lewis and Clark stumbled upon Sacajawea's brother, Cameahwait, who was now chief of the Shoshones. When Sacajawea saw the chief sitting on a white buffalo robe, Clark wrote she "instantly jumped up and ran and embraced him then & threw her blanket over him and cried profusely." She hadn't seen her brother since she had been kidnapped more than five years before. Chief Cameahwait was happy that the white men had kept his sister safe and had treated her well. Lewis and Clark bartered with Cameahwait for 29 horses and one mule, giving him a coat, a pair of scarlet leggings, some

The Continental Divide: "So Long, It's Been Good to Know Ya. . . ."

The spine of the Rocky Mountains is called the Continental Divide because on one side the rivers flow east and on the other, the rivers flow west. Imagine a storm on top of the Rockies. Any rain that falls just west of the highest peaks will flow into rivers heading toward the Pacific Ocean. The rain that falls just east of the highest ridge will flow toward the Mississippi River. For raindrops and for people, the Rockies divide the continent of North America.

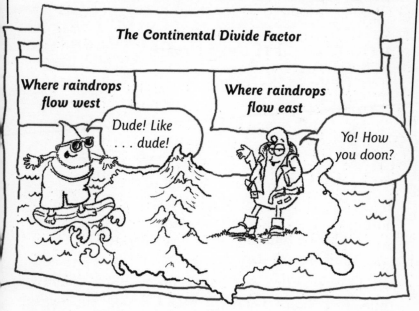

The Continental Divide Factor

Where raindrops flow west

Dude! Like . . . dude!

Where raindrops flow east

Yo! How you doon?

tobacco, knives, and mirrors. Cameahwait agreed to help the Corps of Discovery over the Rocky Mountains, letting them have the services of a Shoshone guide whom the men called Old Toby.

Breaking Wind in History, or The Farts of the Famous

Most history books don't talk too much about history's heroes breaking wind, or farting. But if you've ever been camping with friends, you know it's a fact of life. After barely eating during their trek across the Rockies, the Corps were invited by the Nez Percé to a feast of salmon steaks and vegetable roots. The men all ate too quickly and too much. Clark wrote that he "was so full of wind [he was] scarcely able to breathe."

Tonight I wish we were the plugged nose tribe instead of the pierced nose.

Hey! You guys hear that barking spider? Ha!

Nope! Think I heard buckshot, though.

Uh-oh, bu thunder!

Old Toby told the Corps he could get them over the Continental Divide in four days. Old Toby didn't know what he was talking about. He lost his way. He took the explorers over paths so steep and rocky that the horses rolled backward. Every time they got over a mountain, they'd find another. "I am wet and cold in every part as ever in my life," wrote Clark. Eleven days later, the Corps stumbled out of the Rocky Mountains, more dead than alive. They were on the border of what are now the states of Idaho and Washington. A tribe who called themselves the Nimipu found them. Sacajawea's French-Canadian husband asked them what their name was. In sign language, they kept pointing to their pierced noses, and so became the Nez Percé, which means pierced nose in French.

You Call This Pacific?!

The expedition was headed for the Pacific Ocean on the western side of the Rocky Mountains. It was still hundreds of miles away. The Nez Percé taught the explorers how to make canoes out of huge logs. The Corps of Discovery headed down the Snake River and then into the Columbia River. For the first time on the trip, they were going with the current. They were also traveling over rapids that people pay to go on today.

Soon the Corps found themselves in a very rainy forest in what is now Oregon. Scientists today call this part of the Northwest a temperate rain forest. It's just as wet as the

My name is Meriwether, as in "happy weather." Ironic, huh?

Dude! Surf's totally up! But total bummer: I have hypothermia.

rain forests in South America, but not as hot. The Corps of Discovery made camp on the banks of the Columbia River, a few miles from the Pacific Ocean. The weather was turning cold. Their clothes were rotting from the moisture. Their tents were in tatters.

Finally, on November 18, 1805, Clark left camp, climbed to the top of a hill, and at last saw the Pacific Ocean. The word *pacific* means calm, quiet, and peaceful. But Clark saw a sea foaming with huge waves. Every day was like the last. "I have not seen one Pacific day," complained Clark. "It roars like a repeeted roling thunder." He ended up hating the Pacific for its huge crashing waves that roared in his ears.

Sacajawea was stuck back at camp. One day, word came that there was a beached whale on the coast. Sacajawea wanted to see both the ocean and the whale. So William Clark took her himself.

A Woman and a Black Man Get to Vote

The Corps of Discovery knew they couldn't try to go back over the Rocky Mountains until the spring. Since they were the leaders, Lewis and Clark had to figure out where to spend the winter of 1805–1806. They could have just ordered everybody to make camp wherever they said. But Lewis and Clark put it to a vote instead. They even gave York and Sacajawea a vote. It would be 60 years before a slave such as York would be given a chance to vote in the United States, and a century before women would get to vote. The group decided to stay at a place they named Fort Clatsop after a nearby tribe.

Lewis and Clark Come Home

The winter and early spring of 1806 were miserable, cold, and rainy. Finally, in April of 1806, the Corps of Discovery headed back East. The trip back was no longer an adventure. Everyone just wanted to get home. Lewis was short-tempered, cranky, and depressed — not a good combination. As the expedition passed through tribal territories a second time, the Native Americans wanted more goods for feeding them. When some tribes couldn't get what they wanted, they stole things. One tribe even stole Seaman, Lewis's dog. Lewis said he'd burn down their homes if they didn't give his pet back. The tribe let Seaman go.

When the Corps got back to the Mandan village in North Dakota, they had been gone two years. The group said good-bye to Charbonneau and Sacajawea. Clark promised Sacajawea that when little Pomp was older, he would be happy to educate him as if he were his own son. One Corps of Discovery member, John Colter (see pages 48–49), announced that he didn't want to go back to civilization. He was heading back out West, hoping to make his living as a fur trapper.

What Happened to the Gang

Every white man who had been a member of the Corps of Discovery was rewarded. They each got double pay and land grants for 320 acres apiece.

York got neither pay nor land. He asked for his freedom. Clark said no, because he had grown too used to having him around. Clark complained in a letter that York was getting "uppity and surly." After York married, Clark refused to let him move to Louisville, Kentucky, to live with his wife. Nobody knows exactly what happened to York. One version of York's story says Clark gave him his freedom, but Clark claimed that York couldn't cope with it. York is said to have died in Tennessee from cholera. Another version says a tracker discovered York living with the Crows in Tennessee.

Meriwether Lewis suffered a bad case of writer's block. He took to drinking again and got depressed. In 1809, he killed himself; his last words were "It's hard to die." There were and still are a lot of rumors that he was murdered, but his best friend, William Clark, always believed he committed suicide.

Hey, You're Not Dead!

Lewis and Clark and the rest of the men floated down the Missouri River back to St. Louis. They had been gone two years, four months, and nine days. Most people thought they were dead. Actually, everyone except Sergeant Floyd survived.

William Clark became governor of the Missouri Territory and superintendent for Indian Affairs. He named his son Meriwether Lewis Clark after his best friend, and he made sure that their journals were finally published in 1814. He also became the adoptive father of Sacajawea's son, Pomp. Clark died of natural causes in St. Louis on September 1, 1838.

Sacajawea, her husband, and little Pomp went to live with William Clark in St. Louis a few years after the expedition. When Pomp was about seven years old, Toussaint Charbonneau wanted to go back out West. Sacajawea went with him to South Dakota. According to most reports, she had a baby girl there, named Lisette, and died in 1812. Shoshone stories say Sacajawea lived on and died in 1884, when she would have been about 100 years old. For the story of what happened to Pomp, hold on to your hats! Literally — because the story has to do with hats! (See pages 47–48.)

Just to clarify: When Liz the author writes "People held festive balls in their honor," I'm pretty sure that means fancy parties . . . I'm pretty sure.

When the Corps of Discovery got to St. Louis, almost the entire population came out to greet them. Guns were shot in the air. People stood in line to hear their stories. People held festive balls in their honor.

In late October of 1806, Lewis and Clark led a cavalcade eastward that included Mandan and Osage tribal representatives. The pack train was loaded with whatever "plants, seeds, bird skins, animal skeletons, and furs had not been ruined in water-soaked caches," in addition to their journals and Clark's large map of the American West.

When Meriwether Lewis got to Washington, D.C., he reported in person to the president. Jefferson and Lewis put the maps on the floor of Jefferson's office, and they both got down on their hands and knees to study them. Jefferson couldn't wait for Lewis to edit his journals so they could be published.

When Lewis and Clark's journals were finally published, they became almost instant bestsellers. Everybody wanted to read about the wild lands out West that now belonged to the United States. The

TRAVEL

The years 2004 to 2006 mark the 200th anniversary of Lewis and Clark's expedition. Their entire route has been declared a National Historical Trail through eleven states: Illinois, Missouri, Iowa, Kansas, Nebraska, South Dakota, North Dakota, Montana, Idaho, Oregon, and Washington. You can even visit a replica of **Fort Clatsop**, where the Corps wintered in 1805–1806. It is about five miles southeast of Astoria, Oregon.

explorers' writing was so vivid and full of detail that the journals are still great fun to read today. So if you go on an adventure, keep a journal. You just never know.

Cowabunga, dude!

Check me out! I'm hangin' forty!

Who would have ever thought an ocean whose name means "calm, quiet, and peaceful" would be so loud, fast, and radical?! Apparently, not old William Clark. He was probably just mad because he left his surfboard at home. He should have asked the Native Americans to show him how to make a board out of a tree. That's what I did.

I don't think Clark should be disappointed, though. I mean, look at what an adventure he and Lewis and their posse had. No man had

ever gone where they did. Well, actually, come to think of it, there already were Native American men — and women and children — there, way before the Lewis and Clark show hit town. Still, L&C put the Northwest on the map. In fact, they made the maps.

By the way, it's nice to finally learn who Sacajawea is. I have a bunch of weird-looking gold-colored coins with her picture on them that everybody tells me are worth a dollar.

Oh, well. Now that we know exactly how big America is, I guess we'd better figure out what to do with it all. . . .

Chapter 2
Mountain Men Aren't Pretty

Before Lewis and Clark's expedition, almost nothing was known about the area west of the Mississippi River by anybody except the tribes who lived there. By 1820, so many American citizens had moved into the area around St. Louis, Missouri, that Missouri was ready to become part of the United States. But there was a problem. Would Missouri be admitted as a state that allowed slavery or not?

TIME LINE

1807
John Colter
discovers
Yellowstone

1820
Missouri
Compromise

1825
First mountain
men rendezvous

42

Compromise Is Never Easy

Many people didn't want the territory of the Louisiana Purchase to allow slavery. Slavery had been outlawed in most northern states. Some white people, both in the North and the South, had come to believe that slavery was wrong. Other people didn't want slavery to spread to the newly acquired lands because they didn't want to compete for jobs with people who were forced to work for nothing. Still others didn't want slavery because they were afraid of living near slaves. Ever since the successful slave revolution in Haiti, a lot of people had visions of being murdered in their beds if the slaves in the United States revolted.

On the other hand, most Southerners who moved out West did so with their slaves. They couldn't imagine building a farm without slave labor. Congress had a wild and woolly debate over whether to admit Missouri as a slave state or a free state. Finally, Congress voted that Missouri would come in as a slave state, but in all other states carved out of the Louisiana Purchase, slavery would not be allowed north of the 36°30' parallel. This agreement is called the Missouri Compromise.

1826 to 1838
Trade along the
Santa Fe Trail

1840
Last mountain men
rendezvous

It's All Bunk

There's not much good to be said about the Missouri Compromise, except that we did get the word *bunk* out of it. During the discussions around the compromise, Felix Walker, the representative from Buncombe County, North Carolina, gave a long speech that nobody could make sense of. The word *bunk* came to mean nonsense or talking just to be heard.

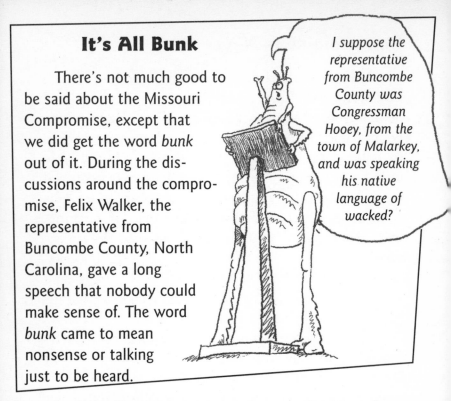

I suppose the representative from Buncombe County was Congressman Hooey, from the town of Malarkey, and was speaking his native language of wacked?

The Missouri Compromise meant that from now on the United States would truly be divided between North and South. Thomas Jefferson wrote, "this question [free state or slave], like a fire bell in the night, awakened and filled me with terror."

Hairy Banknotes

One of the reasons that so many people moved to Missouri was that St. Louis had become a huge marketplace for fur traders, particularly for men selling beaver pelts. Pity the poor beaver, a rather shy rodent that developed its soft, warm, waterproof underbelly of fur so that it could live in very cold mountain streams. It has a fuzzy face, buck teeth, and a paddle for a tail. The odds are good that no beaver ever said to itself, "I want to end up on a tall hat in London." Still, in the 1800s, tall hats made of shaved beaver fur were fashion's latest fad. Everyone who was anyone from London to China and on to Boston wanted one. Beaver pelts became so valuable that they were known as hairy banknotes.

Mad as a Hatter

Workers who made those beaver hats in the 1800s had to treat the beaver fur with mercury to make it soft. The vapors from the mercury could literally drive the workers crazy. That's how the expression "mad as a hatter" came to mean someone who was insane.

Smelly Mountain Men

The first fur trappers who traveled into the territory that Lewis and Clark had charted were known as mountain men. Most of the time you could smell mountain men long before you could see them. They didn't take many baths. Their rifles were kept a lot cleaner than their bodies. They were among the most colorful group of characters that ever existed. There were black trappers, Native American trappers, and white trappers, but

For years I've just been getting dirtier and dirtier. Now with the new Mountain Man Wash, I smell prettier than my grandma on Sunday.

it wasn't the color of their skin that made them colorful. They led a very dangerous life. Most of what these mountain men learned about surviving in the West they picked up from the Native Americans, including the way they dressed.

Fringe Fashion

Western-style shirts with fringes dangling down are still sometimes fashionable. In the 19th century, these fringes weren't just for show. When it rained, the long fringes acted as drains, dripping the water away from the body. The fringes were also handy: They could be used to tie on knives and other tools to keep them close and ready. Mountain men even used the fringes as tourniquets to stop bleeding if necessary. (Trappers were always having accidents.)

The fringes also gave the lice a place to go. Mountain men were forever scratching. If the bugs got on a mountain man's nerves too much, he would take off all his clothes and throw them over an anthill to let the ants eat his lice.

It wasn't just the odor of the mountain men that excited people. Writers and newspaper reporters smelled a good story. People back East couldn't get enough of stories about

Of course, all these old stories are absolutely true.

Tales of the MOUNTAIN MEN

the trappers, alone with their guns and their traps slung over their backs, scaling the rugged mountains. Sometimes, the mountain men didn't even know it, but they were getting nicknames and becoming mighty famous. In fact, many of them are still famous today. Just like Lewis and Clark's journals became best-sellers, so did stories about the mountain men. Here's an all-star cast of mountain men. Just remember: All of them were real people!

Mountain Men All-Stars

Jean-Baptiste "Pomp" Charbonneau (1805–1866)

Pomp, Sacajawea's son, became a mountain man and scout, trapping beaver for those fur hats and helping to map the West. As a boy, Pomp grew up in St. Louis with his adoptive father, William Clark. Clark sent the boy to school in St. Louis. When he was a young adult, Pomp met the German Duke Paul of Württemberg. European royalty were fascinated with all things Native American. The duke

invited Pomp to come live in Europe, which he did until he was 24. When he came back to the United States in 1829, he worked as a guide and mountain man. Pomp was famous for reciting Shakespeare around mountain campfires. He died of an illness on his way to a gold rush in Montana in 1866.

John "Run for Your Life" Colter (c. 1775–1813)

After leaving the Lewis and Clark expedition, John Colter went back to Wyoming with his rifle and a 30-pound pack. In the winter of 1807, he stumbled into what he thought looked like burning vapors from caves. Most people thought Colter was drunk or making up stories about what he saw. They called the place he told them about Colter's Hell,

and they didn't believe it existed. Later, some Blackfeet caught Colter and his partner, John Potts, trapping on their land. Potts was killed and Colter was stripped naked and told to run. The Blackfeet chased after him. Totally buck naked, Colter ran and walked about 200 miles. After 11 days, he stumbled into the stockade at Fort Raymond, Wyoming, more dead than alive. He still didn't want to give up his life as a mountain man. He signed on to lead another fur trading party in 1810. Once again, the Blackfeet attacked them. Finally, Colter had had enough. He used the money he made in the fur trade to buy a plot of land in Missouri. The Blackfeet couldn't kill him, but illness could. He died of jaundice in 1813, when he was 38.

Hugh "Grizzlies Can't Kill Me" Glass (177?–1833)

Historians don't know where or when Hugh Glass was born. He just showed up in the Rockies as a

trapper for the Rocky Mountain Fur Company. One August day in 1823, while trapping with some friends, Glass got a hankering for some berries. Unfortunately, so did a mother grizzly bear with two cubs. The mama bear charged, tore Glass's throat open, and ripped his shoulder to the bone. Then she bit a chunk out of his thigh to take back to her cubs. Glass lost consciousness. Most of his friends were sure he would die by morning and wanted to leave him. But 19-year-old Jim Bridger and an older friend, John S. Fitzgerald, said they'd stay to bury him. But tough Hugh Glass didn't die. After Glass was in a coma for five days, Bridger and Fitzgerald left him for dead and took his rifle. When Glass woke up, he was so mad that he had been left alone to die that he swore he'd kill the men who left him. He dragged himself for nearly 150 miles. When he finally caught up with young Jim Bridger, he decided to forgive him because he was just a kid. So he went after Fitzgerald. He called Fitzgerald a no-good coward and got his rifle back, but he never did kill any of the men who left him. Hugh Glass died ten years later in a fight with the Arikara tribe of North Dakota.

Jim "Old Gabe" Bridger (1804–1881)

Jim Bridger became known as Old Gabe because he lived longer than any of the other mountain men. He had a great sense of humor, loving to tease newcomers, or tenderfeet, telling them tall tales, such as that he was so old he could remember when Pikes Peak was just a hole in the ground.

Bridger was once shot in the back with an arrow and didn't have anyone to take the arrowhead out for three years. When Dr. Whitman, a missionary, took the arrowhead out, he couldn't believe Bridger's back wasn't infected. "Meat jes don't spoil in the mountains," Bridger said.

Bridger was one of the ablest of the mountain men both as a trapper and as a scout. The maps he drew with charcoal on buffalo skin were the best maps in the West.

Bridger was also the first white man to see the Great Salt Lake in what is now Utah, and he discovered the south pass, which would become part of the Oregon Trail, the easiest way to get over the Rockies. From 1824 until the late 1860s, Bridger worked in the West, making a living as a beaver trapper, guide, and storekeeper. He guided more wagon trains than all other scouts put together. With Louis Vasquez, he founded Fort Bridger, on the Oregon Trail, in 1843. In 1855, he bought a farm south of Kansas City on State Line Road. He died on the farm in 1881, when he was 77 and blind, one of the last of the mountain men.

James "Gaudy Liar" Beckwourth (1798–1866)
Jim Beckwourth was born in Virginia. His father was a white Revolutionary War veteran; his mother was an African-American slave. His father wanted to raise him as a free man, but because his mother was a slave, Beckwourth was considered a slave, too. The family moved to St. Louis and Beckwourth became an apprentice to a blacksmith. Beckwourth didn't like life as an apprentice, and he ran away to the West. He became a fur trapper and hunter, famous for his tall tales. In 1828, when Beckwourth was about 30 years old, one of his friends got him to play a practical joke on Chief Big Bowl of the Crow tribe. Beckwourth claimed to be the chief's missing

child. What started as a practical joke turned out to be great for Beckwourth. He was treated better than he had ever been in his life. He was given the choice of three beautiful sisters for a bride, and he lived in Montana as a Crow for six to eight years.

Beckwourth eventually left the Crows, wandered back East and fought in Florida, and then headed for California. In 1851, while working for General John C. Frémont, Beckwourth discovered a pass through the Northern Sierra that bears his name today. There are also a mountain, valley, and town in California that bear his name. He died in 1866. According to some legends he was poisoned, either by a tribe who was angry that he hadn't returned to be their chief, or by his wife.

Jedidiah "Clean as a Whistle" Strong Smith (1799–1831)

Jedidiah Strong Smith was very different from most mountain men. He didn't drink alcohol or swear, and he took baths. He was a crack shot and tough as a bear. Once a grizzly attacked him and took most of one of his ears, but Smith somehow got the bear to spit it out. Smith got a friend to sew the ear back on. From then on, Smith wore his hair long to hide the scar. Jedidiah Strong Smith wandered all the way to California, crossing the Sierra Nevada from west to east and vice versa, stopping in what is now Las Vegas. But Smith would probably not like the bright lights that he'd find in

Las Vegas now. He'd probably take off again to be on his own. (For how he died on the Santa Fe Trail, see page 60.)

Kit Carson (1809–1868)

Like Jedidiah Strong Smith, Kit Carson was unusual because he was as "clean as a hound's tooth," according to one acquaintance, and a man whose "word was as sure as the sun comin' up." Carson didn't talk much, but he never backed down from a fight, and he was said to be as brave a man as ever lived. He operated out of Taos, New Mexico, and his fur trapping took him as far west as California. He traveled and lived among Native Americans, and his first two wives were Arapaho and Cheyenne women. He became one of the most trustworthy of scouts and would later lead John C. Frémont and American troops to conquer California.

Carson fought in the Civil War, in which New Mexico was on the Confederate side, but most of his fighting during that war was against the Navajo. After the Civil War, he moved to Colorado, and he died there in 1868. His remains were brought back to a small cemetery near his old home in Taos, New Mexico.

Mike "Ring-tailed Roarer" Fink (1770?–1823)

Mike Fink was the least trustworthy of the mountain men, and his name has entered the language as someone who can't be trusted.

Mountain Men Lingo: It's a Blast!

Like the word *fink,* we sometimes still use slang that comes to us from the mountain men, and we don't even know it.

Hungry as a wolf

Make tracks When you had to move fast; named after the tracks you left in the snow or mud.

Rubbed out Getting killed either by an accident or in a fight.

Have a blast If a mountain man didn't get rubbed out, you could bet that he would show up for the mountain men rendezvous and have a "blast," or a wild time. Have a blast is thought to come from the sound of guns going off in the air. It's something that would happen quite often when the mountain men got together.

Fink was one of the best river rafters on the fast-flowing rivers of the Rockies. Words flowed out of his mouth just as fast and so did bullets from his rifle. He got the nickname Ring-tailed Roarer because he supposedly once shot and hit the tails of eight piglets on shore, some 40 or 50 yards away. Fink liked to go into taverns and shout, "Whoo-oop! . . . Look at me! I'm the man they call Sudden Death and General Desolation!"

One day, Mike Fink got in a fight with two friends (there's some dispute about whether the fight was over a woman or over some beaver pelts). Fink pretended to make up and suggested they play a friendly game of Shoot a Cup of Whiskey Off

If you're hungry as a wolf and you want to have a blast make tracks to the

MOUNTAIN MAN RONDEVOO

WHERE: the misty clearing by Big Stink Lake

WHEN: The snow melts

(you'll feel like a Fink if you miss it)

Each Other's Heads from 60 Yards. The friend, who Fink thought was cheating him, put a glass on his head. Fink shot him between the eyes. Fink claimed it was an accident, but everyone knew that Mike Fink was a sure shot. When Fink's other friend realized it couldn't have been an accident, he shot Fink dead, but Fink's legend lives on. Out West, one of the worst things you could call anyone was a "fink" — it means that person couldn't be trusted and might rat out a good friend. Now you know where the word came from.

Party Hardy! Mountain Men Rendezvous

During the summer months, the beavers shed their fur, so it wasn't a good time to trap them. Instead, mountain men got together to party hardy!

Every summer, the traders from St. Louis and other towns would set up a date and place for mountain men to gather and trade their pelts. These meetings were called *rendezvous,* after the French words meaning "present yourselves." Sometimes more than a thousand trappers showed up, along with hundreds, if not thousands, of Native Americans from many different tribes. The trappers and the Native Americans gambled all night with the traders from the big cities. It wasn't unusual for a mountain man to lose all his money. The traders loved to see the trappers gamble

Ironically, the less-skilled mountain men were often the ones found to be outstanding in their fields.

Hello . . . mountain men? Hello? Dang! This is the only stinky lake I know.

TRAVEL

Both **Fort Bridger** (founded by Jim Bridger) and **Jackson Hole** in Wyoming re-create the mountain men rendezvous every summer. Fort Bridger's celebration is held on Labor Day weekend, Jackson Hole's is always in June.

because if they lost money, they'd be desperate to sell their furs cheap.

Careful of the Calabozo, or Life on the Santa Fe Trail

At least the mountain men in the North were in United States territory bought by the Louisiana Purchase. The fur trappers in the Southwest were in Spanish territory. If they were caught they could be stuck in a dungeon or *calabozo*. "Calaboose" is still western slang for jail.

In 1821, Mexico won independence from Spain. The Mexicans in Santa Fe were hungry for goods from the United States. Soon, mountain men like Kit Carson discovered that they could make more money guiding traders to Santa Fe than they could as fur trappers. The 800-mile trek between Independence, Missouri, and Santa Fe became a major trade route. American traders loved going to Santa Fe. They particularly liked the señoritas at the dances. Traders had to get used to one local Santa Fe practice, however. If you wanted to attract

someone of the oppo-
site sex, you broke an
eggshell filled with
cologne over his or
her head.

I'll tell you, Santa Fe is no place where you want to be pretty.

Do You Know the Way to Santa Fe?

The 800 miles
between Independence,
Missouri, and Santa Fe,
New Mexico, were full of deserts and rough territory little known by white people. Pawnee, Osages,
Arapaho, Kiowa, and the Comanche, the most
feared tribe of them all, hunted bison on this land
and considered it their own. Mostly the tribes did
their own trading with the Santa Fe wagon trains,
but occasionally hostilities broke out. So, when the

Mind Your *P*'s and *Q*'s

Spring was a wild time in Independence, Missouri,
when the Santa Fe traders got ready to take off. Bartenders
warned their patrons to mind their pints and quarts or "*p*'s
and *q*'s." In other words, don't drink too much. So if anyone tells you to "mind your *p*'s and *q*'s," remind them that
you're not old enough to drink alcohol, anyhow.

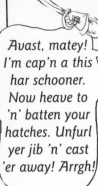

Avast, matey! I'm cap'n a this har schooner. Now heave to 'n' batten your hatches. Unfurl yer jib 'n' cast 'er away! Arrgh!

Jedidiah Strong Smith Makes a Wrong Turn

In the first ten years, only eight white people were killed in attacks on the wagon trains to Santa Fe. One of them was mountain man Jedidiah Strong Smith. In 1831, when he was just 32 years old, Smith agreed to lead his own caravan to Santa Fe. He knew the northern Rockies like the back of his hand, but he didn't know the southern territory. He got lost while crossing the Cimarron Desert in southwestern Kansas, an area of 50 miles of soft sand without a drop of water. His caravan ran out of water. Smith said he would find the Cimarron River himself. He did, but the Comanche found him and thought he was invading their land. They scalped him and left his body for the buzzards. Because of incidents like that, nobody wanted to go on the Santa Fe Trail alone.

Tell you what. Let's elect ourselves another leader and this time let's not call him captain.

Bent's Old Fort National Historic Site near La Junta, Colorado, is a reconstruction of a trading post that greeted travelers along the Santa Fe Trail. **Santa Fe, New Mexico,** still has many historic buildings and a Saturday market that re-creates the atmosphere of the boom days along the Santa Fe Trail. You can also visit Kit Carson's home and museum in Taos, New Mexico.

wagon trains moved out, they traveled in a square, making the wagons into a moving fort.

Most of the wagons that white folks used on the Oregon Trail were first test-driven on the Santa Fe Trail. These wagons were called prairie schooners because their canvas tops looked like sails in the prairie grass. The wheels were painted bright colors so they could be seen in the dust.

Each wagon train elected a captain. The captain decided what route to take, when to go, and where to camp.

The wagons were mostly pulled by oxen and led by men called bullwhackers, who guided the team. "Ho-haw" meant turn left; "geeho" meant turn right. "Whoa" meant stop. A bullwhacker walked alongside his team with a "Missouri pistol," a whip that sounded like a pistol shot when it was snapped. He didn't use the whip to beat his oxen — they were too valuable for that — but the sound of the snapping whip made them move. The whips were also useful for killing rattlesnakes and for punishing humans, who weren't considered as valuable as the oxen. If somebody got out of hand or stole something, they could be tied to a wagon wheel and whipped.

The End of the Beaver Trade

Fashions change. While the mountain men were whooping it up at their rendezvous, people in London and Paris suddenly decided that they wanted hats made from the spit of caterpillars. Silk, made from the cocoons of worms turning into butterflies, became the new fashion. Suddenly, everyone wanted a silk hat. Beaver hats were out. The last real mountain men rendezvous took place in 1840.

I'm telling you, Caleb, mountain men are out! Trappers are out! Worm wrangler! That's where the money is! Oh, no! Run for your life! Stampede!

How can you tell?

Now many mountain men were out of work. Some moved back East. Some, like Kit Carson and Jedidiah Strong Smith, tried to make it as guides on the Santa Fe Trail. But up North, in the mountain men's traditional territory, new folks were coming from back East. They weren't coming for beaver. They were coming to stay. And the mountain men would find jobs guiding them across the mountains.

Those mountain men

sure were some tough characters, weren't they? And they were as messy as they were tough. Here's a story about a creature who dared to clean up the mess the mountain men left behind. His name was Samuel "Dances with Food Scraps" Roach.

Legend has it, one day Dances with Food Scraps was doing what he did best: eatin' his way through an old pile of food scraps. Suddenly, he heard a great *Roar!!!* and looked up to see a gigantic bear. Now, this bear didn't just swat at Dances with

Food Scraps' neck, or take a bite out of his leg, or merely chew his ear off. This bear was soooo hungry that with one huge bite, he gobbled up all the food scraps and scarfed up Samuel right along with them. Swallowed that ole roach whole!

Now, Dances with Food Scraps was so tough that he actually stayed alive in that bear's belly for three days and lived to tell about it! (Don't ask how. It's really gross. Even grosser is how he escaped!)

But, back to the book. When we left off, Americans were itching to go west. But just because they knew the way didn't mean the going wasn't going to be tough. . . .

Chapter 3
Goin' West to Settle Down

When President Jefferson bought the Louisiana Purchase, he had a dream of white small-farm owners from the United States moving into it and settling down with the Native American tribes who already lived there. The first people from the East who *did* move into the Louisiana Territory to settle down were actually Native Americans themselves. They came from the Choctaw, Cherokee, Chickasaw, Creek, and Seminole tribes. They sure didn't go peacefully, and they sure didn't go because they wanted a better

TIME LINE

1830
President Andrew Jackson signs the Indian Removal Act

1836
Narcissa Whitman and Eliza Spaulding become the first white women to cross the Rockies

1838
Cherokee Trail of Tears

66

life. Most of them went because a gun with a bayonet was pointed at them.

The Cherokee, Farmers of the Southeast

Ever since colonial days, white people had been moving onto land that had been lived on for generations by Native Americans, and then telling the tribes to get "civilized." In other words, to live like white people. As the Cherokee elder, Corn Tassel, asked in 1785, "May we not ask why the white people do not hunt and live as we do?"

The Cherokee had always farmed the rich lands of the South. By the 1820s, some of them had become wealthy plantation owners and owned slaves. The Cherokee developed a written language and wrote a constitution for their nation.

Nunahi-Duna-Dlo-Hilu-I: Trail Where They Cried

Gold was discovered on Cherokee land in Georgia around 1828. Hundreds of white miners

1841
First covered wagons on the Oregon Trail

1847
Mormons settle Utah

swarmed there. It didn't matter how "civilized" the Cherokee were or what treaties they had signed, once gold was discovered, white people wanted the Cherokee land. The idea of getting rid of the Cherokee and moving them out into the

Andrew "Old Hickory" Jackson (1767–1845)

In 1828, Andrew Jackson from Tennessee became the first president elected who was from one of the new states. Until then, every president had come from either Virginia or Massachusetts.

As a kid, Jackson was a lot to handle. When he was a teenager, he loved to play practical jokes like moving outhouses in the middle of the night. When people got up to go to the bathroom, they couldn't find the bathroom.

You can see Jackson's picture on a $20 bill. His blazing eyes (they're blue but they show up black on the $20 bill) glare out at you. It wasn't a good idea to get Jackson

Louisiana Purchase seemed like a great idea to many white people.

On May 28, 1830, President Andrew Jackson signed the Indian Removal Act, declaring that the tribes in the Southeast had to leave their homes and move to Oklahoma. No tribe felt more betrayed

angry, but it wasn't hard to do. He was involved in as many as 103 duels. He especially hated it if anybody said anything bad about his beloved wife, Rachel. Andrew Jackson won fame as an Indian fighter in the South. Yet he adopted a Creek baby boy, Lyncoya, and raised him as his own. He found the baby on the battlefield while he was fighting against the Creeks in the South. But for most Native Americans, Andrew Jackson was their worst nightmare.

Sir! I say, sir! This combo meal has not been super-sized! You offend my honor, sir. I demand satisfaction! Pistols at dawn, sir!

Umm. . . can I give you a yummy-o-pie puff instead?

Okay.

My honor is satisfied, sir. Can it be cherry?

Yeah!

The Andrew Jackson School of Conflict Negotiation

Talking Leaves and the Sequoia Trees

By the 19th century, people with a written language had the upper hand, especially when they forced other people to sign "treaties." This point wasn't lost on many Native American tribes. Many of the tribes learned to speak English, but there was no way to write down their own language. Then a Cherokee, Sequoyah, and his young daughter, Ayoka, found a way to put the Cherokee language into symbols. Ayoka was particularly good at helping her father pick out sounds. The language became known as "talking leaves." In 1907 when Oklahoma became a state, the citizens wanted to call the state "Sequoyah," but Congress overruled them. However, the name Sequoyah lives on. The giant California redwood trees are called sequoia after the Cherokee who invented the written Cherokee language.

Hey! Where is everybody?

Aahhh!

Why am I the opposite of Mozart?

I don't know, why?

He was a composer, I'm a decomposer. Ha! Leaf humor!

Ow! Ow! Ow!

Boy, I sure hope he hasn't been drinking.

If Leaves Really Could Talk

than the Cherokee. All of a sudden it didn't matter that they had a constitution and treaties giving them the right to their land.

The Cherokee nation took their case to the Supreme Court. They even won one of their cases. President Jackson didn't care. He sneered that the Supreme Court didn't have any troops, but he did. In 1838, the United States Army began rounding up the Cherokee. A few Cherokee escaped to the hills and stayed behind, but some 16,000 people were penned up in log stockades all summer, where many got sick and died. When the remaining Cherokee were forced to make the 800-mile walk to Oklahoma, in October of 1838, a cold autumn rain fell all along the way. By March of 1839, all the survivors arrived in Oklahoma; some 4,000 Cherokee had died.

The Cherokee and the Creeks were forced to settle on dry, desertlike land in Oklahoma that

As roaches go, I'm fairly funny, but sometimes I have to admit, it gets hard to make jokes.

In 1987, Congress established the **Trail of Tears National Historic Trail.** It is 2,200 miles of land and water routes. You can follow the official trail markers and visit many trail sites.

wasn't very good for farming. But they tried. When the Cherokee got to Oklahoma, they immediately began to build churches, schools, and printing presses. Their land in Oklahoma became the first towns settled by easterners in the West.

Meet the Missionaries, a Soap Opera From the 19th Century

As a teenager in New York State, Narcissa Prentiss was known for her blond good looks and her beautiful singing voice. She could have married many times. Instead, when she was just 16 years old, she decided she wanted to be a Presbyterian missionary out West. But the American Board of Commissioners of Foreign Missions wouldn't send a woman alone. Then Narcissa met Marcus Whitman, a doctor who also wanted to go west to save souls. Narcissa and Marcus got married and headed west. Unfortunately, the missionary board chose Henry Harmon Spaulding (one of Narcissa's former suitors) and his new wife, Eliza, to go west, too. Henry had never forgiven Narcissa for turning down his earlier marriage proposal. He still hated her and thought she was an empty-headed fool. But the Spauldings and the Whitmans headed west together, anyhow.

Tea on the Trail

In St. Louis, the Spauldings and the Whitmans bought wagons like those that had been test-driven on the Santa Fe Trail. The journey from St. Louis, Missouri, to the Rockies was probably the happiest time of Narcissa's life. Most of the way, she rode her horse sidesaddle. Almost every day, the two couples stopped at noon for lunch despite the fact that they were hurrying to catch up with a fur company's trade caravan. When they did catch up, Narcissa invited the mountain men to tea with her and used her good china. The mountain men often went years without seeing a white woman. The Spauldings were shocked. They thought Narcissa was being forward, but she had a grand time.

As they began the trek over the Rocky Mountains, the trip became harder. The Whitmans had to get rid of Narcissa's trunk of clothes and some of their books. As they crossed the Rockies, they began to run into the Native Americans they were planning to convert. Narcissa was upset that the shy, sickly Eliza Spaulding did better with most Native Americans than she did.

Missionary Life Isn't All Tea and Cookies

When the Whitmans and Spauldings arrived in Oregon, things had gotten so nasty between the two couples that they split up. Narcissa wrote that she was shocked that Oregon was so different from what she thought it would be. She thought they were going into a wilderness, but instead they were surrounded by farms, some run by British mountaineers who had settled in with Native American wives, some run by the Native Americans themselves.

The Whitmans ended up on the Walla Walla River in the Willamette Valley, among the Cayuse people, who had farmed the area for centuries. The Whitmans tried to convert the Cayuse to Christianity, but they wouldn't allow the Cayuse into their house. The chief of the Cayuse was insulted when

Narcissa didn't invite him into her parlor to worship. Narcissa wrote that the "Indians said they'd worship in our new house, but if they did [they'd be] so dirty and full of fleas [we] couldn't live in it. . . ."

Oregon Fever: It's Like Texas Fever but with More Rain

As miserable as Narcissa was with the Cayuse, she and her husband wrote glowing reports of their life in Oregon. Perhaps they didn't want to admit how lonely they were. People back East published the letters from Oregon, touting how green and beautiful everything was. Rumors spread that you could pull vegetables right out of the ground in Oregon, practically as soon as you planted them.

Like the exploits of mountain men, the qualities of Oregon were slightly exaggerated back East.

Hang on, honey. It takes about seven minutes to grow a BLT.

In 1837, the American economy was in the dumps. Things were going from bad to worse for people back East. Oregon, even though it didn't officially belong to the United States, looked good to many people. In June of 1843, about a thousand Americans took off from Independence, Missouri, in approximately 120 covered wagons, with around 4,000 cattle and oxen. They got to Oregon in November without much trouble. The next year, more than 2,000 people took off for Oregon. By 1846, there were nearly 9,000 Americans in Oregon. By that time, the beaver was almost wiped out. In 1846, Great Britain and the United States made a treaty settling the United States and Canadian boundary at the 49th parallel. Americans started heading west by wagon in even greater numbers.

There was often death and hardship on the trail to the West, but the amazing thing is many

Keep Your Journal

Most of the people who went on the Oregon Trail, especially women and children, looked at this as the great adventure of their lives. They wrote journals or letters to their friends. In their book *Frontier Children* (University of Oklahoma Press), Linda Peavy and Ursula Smith gathered many of the journals that children wrote. Most of the quotes from this section come from their book. So here, mostly straight from children's journals, is a little slice of life on the Oregon Trail.

kids felt like D. B. Ward, who wrote, "For me, a lad of fifteen, it was the most interesting period of my life." Thirteen-year-old Martha Edgarton Plassman wrote, "There were no regrets on my part at leaving my relatives and my native town. It meant for me adventure."

Anybody for a Game of Buffalo Chips?

Buffalo chips are dried mounds of buffalo poop. The good thing about the poop was that when it dried, it had enough gas in it to burn cleanly. Once dry, it didn't even stink. "Gathering buffalo chips was Ester's and my job," nine-year-old Florence Weeks wrote. "We were rather finicky about it at first but found that they were as dry as a chip of weed. We had a basket with a handle on each side to carry them." Jesse Applegate made the chore into a game of who could make the biggest pile. Nine-year-old Henry Brown remembers getting his seven-year-old sister, Mary Jane, to guard the family's chips against raids from other children.

Oh, my goodness! These chips taste like cr

Crispy.

Child's Play

The pioneer kids had a lot more energy than the adults. Children loved catching crickets and, just like Lewis and Clark, trying to catch prairie dogs. When the wagon train made camp, kids played games like tag and hide-and-seek.

The Stinky Trail

Most wagon trains started out in the spring but the weather soon got hot. Imagine sweating day after day, but never taking a bath or shower. And this was before the days of T-shirts and shorts. Women wore long dresses, for the most part, and men wore long pants. There wasn't much changing of clothes. The travelers wore the same clothes day after day. Could it get any worse? Yes. They often had no choice but to drink stagnant water that was full of germs, which had the inevitable result: diarrhea. For many settlers, this was a chronic condition. At least the mountain men traveled

I think he finally just smelled so bad, he turned completely into stink and just blew away.

alone, for the most part. The wagon trains had hundreds of stinking men, women, and children all together. Most native tribes who met the wagon train folks couldn't take the smell. Native Americans, who bathed regularly, thought these white people were uncivilized because of their poor hygiene.

It was just incredibly filthy on the trail. The mosquitoes would eat you alive. If it was dry, the dust was so bad that it would get in your ears, hair, and mouth. If it was muddy, it was even worse because the oxen would have to pull the heavy wagons through the mud.

Give an Ox a Moccasin

Oxen pulled most wagons. Horses were too delicate to do the heavy pulling. Mules were tough, but they were stubborn and sometimes wouldn't move. Oxen were strong and usually willing to go along. But oxen were fussy eaters and had delicate feet. Their feet were so tender that most people in wagon trains put moccasins on them to protect their hooves.

Son, this family has worn oxfords for generations. You are going to wear a pair of oxfords, too.

But, Dad! All the guys are calling me "oxymoron."

There was no padding either along the wheels or inside the wagons. The trail was so bumpy that almost everybody found it much more comfortable to walk or ride a horse than to stay inside the wagon. The oxen only went about three miles an hour, so it was easy to keep up. (This author took a wagon train to see what it was like, and believe me, you'd rather walk, even in the dust.)

Tribes and Wagon Trains

During the years 1840 to 1850, very few people on wagon trains even saw Native Americans, and when they did, there were very few hostile acts. The Native Americans considered the whites as people "moving through" their territory, not permanent residents. Most tribes along the route traded with the wagon trains or charged tolls for help getting them across rivers. This didn't stop kids from telling each other horror stories around the campfire. Kids liked to scare themselves with scary stories about running into Native Americans. Few kids actually ever met any. When the kids on the wagon trains did encounter tribal people, they were surprised that most Native Americans were cleaner than they were.

As for what the Native Americans thought of the whites, there are far fewer journals. But Sarah Winnemucca, the daughter of a Paiute chief in what is now Nevada, wrote, "What a fright we all got one morning to hear some white people were

Looky here, Ma! People 'round here just come growing up out of the ground.

coming. My aunt said to my mother, 'Let us bury our girls or they shall be killed.' So our mothers buried me and my cousin, planted sage bushes over our faces to keep the sun from burning them . . . [until the whites passed]."

Death on the Trail

When people died on the trail, they were buried quickly. Usually, there wasn't even enough wood to make a coffin. The wagons would run over the graves so that the passing wheels would pack the earth down and save the bodies from raids by wolves and grave robbers. For the children on the wagon trains, death became something they got used to as long as it didn't happen to their loved ones.

Despite the good cheer of so many of the journals, the trip west was dangerous, not because of Native Americans, but because of sickness and accidents. The wagons had to be pulled across dangerous rivers. Many more people drowned crossing

The Death of Narcissa Whitman

The Oregon Trail brought the wagon trains close to the Whitmans' homestead. In 1844, Narcissa took in seven orphans, the Sager children. Their parents had died on the Oregon Trail.

In 1847, an epidemic of measles hit the Cayuse, killing half of them. Marcus Whitman tried to nurse the sick, but when the Cayuse chief's child died, the chief blamed the Whitmans. There had been bad blood between them for years. Three Cayuse, including the chief, came to the Whitmans' house and shot and hacked Marcus Whitman to death. Narcissa dragged her husband's body into the house and tried to calm the children. One of the Native Americans shot her through the glass door. The ball from the musket shattered the glass and entered her shoulder. Narcissa kept praying over and over, "Lord, save these little ones." The Cayuse entered the house and spared some of the young orphans, but they carried out the wounded Narcissa and killed her.

Boy, nothing but a whole bunch of depressing stuff all over this page. Keep reading. It's got to lighten up.

the rivers than from Native American attacks. The biggest cause of death was cholera, a disease that comes from drinking bad water.

The Mormons Move West

There was a group of religious people who traveled out West that didn't go to convert the Native Americans. The Mormons went to escape religious persecution themselves. In the 1830s, there were many new religious groups in the United States. The founder of the Mormon religion, Joseph Smith, discovered what he said was a set of hammered gold plates in upstate New York, not far from Buffalo. Smith said these plates told the story of one of the lost tribes of Israel that had wandered to the shores of the New World. Smith's followers called themselves the Church of Jesus Christ of Latter Day Saints, or the Mormons.

Smith imagined a "New Jerusalem," a place where Mormons would be safe to live life without interference from others. In 1839, Smith and his followers moved to southern Illinois to the tiny town of Nauvoo. They began work on a huge temple. By 1844, Nauvoo had a population of more than 12,000. It was the biggest and richest city in the state, far bigger than Chicago or any other city in the Midwest.

The Mormons viewed themselves as the chosen people. They were hardworking and prosperous but kept their distance from others. They held a number of beliefs that rubbed many people the wrong way. They were antislavery in a time and place where most people supported slavery. Joseph Smith believed that the patriarchs of the Mormon Church could and should take more than one wife. That was against the law in most states. Not all Mormons agreed with Smith on this issue. In 1844, Smith tried to shut down the printing press of

Captain Pitt's Brass Band

The Mormons were the only group to travel with their own band. Captain Pitt's Brass Band was a band from England whose musicians had all converted to Mormonism. They played along the entire 1,300-mile journey. When the Mormons reached a town, the brass band often played a concert for the townspeople as a way to make money. The West had never seen anything like it. The Mormons believed music and dancing would keep their spirits up.

some Mormons who disagreed with him. Fighting broke out and Smith, along with his brother, was taken to a jail in nearby Carthage, Illinois. There, an angry anti-Mormon mob broke into Smith's cell and murdered him and his brother.

One of Smith's followers, Brigham Young, became the new leader of the Mormons. Young decided to move his people and all their belongings somewhere so far away that no one would bother them. He had heard rumors of a huge lake full of salt water somewhere in the middle of the Rocky Mountains.

At that time, Utah was an isolated area, home to the Pueblos, Paiutes, Ute, and Shoshones. In theory it was owned by Mexico, but almost no Spaniards or Mexicans lived there. There were very few American citizens, either. Young thought Utah would be the perfect place for the Mormons — if he could find it. There were very few maps of the area, and Young had just a vague idea of exactly where this salt lake was.

In February 1846, 1,600 Mormons headed west across the Mississippi. They moved slowly across Iowa, and spent the winter camped out in present-day Omaha, Nebraska, and Council Bluffs, Iowa.

Then, in April 1847, Brigham Young set off with his Pioneer Band. His mission was to find a place for all the Mormons to settle. He took off with 143 men, 3 women, and 2 children, in 72 wagons, with 93 horses, 77 oxen, 52 mules, 19 cows, and flocks of chickens.

Young ordered the Mormons still in winter camp to get ready to make the trip after him. The Mormons would run the best-organized wagon trains in the West. Each family had to have exactly six oxen. Groups of 50 families banded together. Dogs had to be kept leashed, and there was a lost and found. Each day started with the sound of the trumpet and ended with the ringing of the temple bell.

On July 24, 1847, Brigham Young and the Pioneer Band of Mormons entered the valley of the Great Salt Lake. "This is the place," Young is said to have declared. Within days, Young planned streets 132 feet wide in great square blocks. The city was laid out. By September, more than 5,000 Mormons had arrived. Over the next 22 years, some 70,000 Mormons walked or came in wagon trains. Their New Jerusalem became Salt Lake City and the state of Utah.

Mormon Pioneer National Historic Trail and **Salt Lake City.** The general route is from Nauvoo, Illinois, to Salt Lake City, Utah. This 1,300-mile trail passes through Illinois, Iowa, Nebraska, Wyoming, and Utah, with many historic sites, including the Historic Nauvoo Visitors Center in Nauvoo, Illinois, and the Historic Winter Quarters in Omaha, Nebraska. In Salt Lake City, the Daughters of the Utah Pioneers offers a museum and archives containing many artifacts and documents related to early Utah settlement and the Mormon Trail. The Museum of Church History and Art contains many original works of art and artifacts related to the Mormon pioneers.

Can you imagine

walking from Illinois all the way to Utah?!
That's like walking to school and back, like,
a hundred gazillion times! No, thank you!
I can't even make it from one end of the
kitchen to the other, unless there are plenty
of crumbs to eat along the way. And even
then, I need a few days to rest up before
I even think about going back.

I'll tell you one thing, though — these

covered wagons are so uncomfortable, it's not much better than walking. My butt is killing me! Thank goodness we stop at nightfall. Nothing like a little barbecue, singing, and storytelling 'round the campfire. Plus, it's so dark these humans don't know what they're dropping.

Aside from the long walk, the bumpy ride, and the smelly people — who are so smelly I can barely stand it — the West doesn't seem quite as tough as I thought it would be. Of course, we haven't been to Texas yet.

Chapter 4
Howdy, Texas!

Texas! The very word came from a mix-up. In the 1600s, when the Spaniards first arrived in the northeast of what we now call Texas, they used sign language to try to ask the native Hasinai tribe what their name was. *"Teychas! Teychas!"* the Hasinai shouted, which meant *friend* in their language; it was *not* their name. From then on, Spaniards called the place *Tejas*. In old Spanish, the *x* was used to make a *j* sound, so sometimes it was spelled Texas. Confused? Texas has been confusing people for hundreds of years!

For 317 years, Texas was part of Mexico, but it was much closer to the United States than it was to

TIME LINE

1821
Moses Austin makes a deal to come to Texas

1832
Sam Houston arrives; Texans talk independence

1836
Battle of the Alamo; Texas wins its independence from Mexico

90

Mexico City. By the 1820s, many American citizens were crossing the border into Texas illegally and just daring Mexico to try to catch them and kick them out.

A Mustanger Loses an Ear

The first American citizens who crossed into Texas went to capture wild horses. They called themselves mustangers. The Spaniards called them pirates. In 1801, the Spaniards caught Philip Nolan, a mustanger. They shot him and cut off his ears. They hoped that would teach Americans to stay on their side of the

Philip Nolan Finds Shakespeare's **Julius Caesar** *Uncomfortable*

1836 to 1845
Texas is an independent republic

border. It didn't. The mustangers continued to cross over.

Mexico won its independence from Spain in 1821. Texas was now part of the new independent Republic of Mexico. Mexico was a huge country that stretched from what is today California and Texas, down to the borders of Central America.

You would think two new baby republics, both having fought a revolutionary war against a European "mother country," would be friends. But the United States did little to help Mexico win its fight against Spain. Mexico went through a period of chaos during and after its war for independence, just as the United States had. During that time, Americans looked across their border, saw Mexican land, and said to themselves, "Let's go get it."

Inviting the Fox into the Chicken Coop

Foxes love to eat chickens. Inviting a fox into a chicken coop is an old expression for inviting a bully to take a bite of your candy bar. Chances are the bully will take the whole thing. And that's what happened to the new Republic of Mexico in the 1820s.

The new independent government in Mexico City didn't know what to do about all the illegal aliens from the United States swarming across its border into Texas. Moses Austin, an American from Missouri, promised Mexico that he would get Americans to give up their United States citizenship and become Mexican citizens.

In 1821, Mexico agreed to Austin's scheme. Austin promised that his Americans would not only become Mexican citizens, they would even fight for Mexico against foreigners — that is, the United States. Austin also promised that his group would become Roman Catholic, the religion of almost all Spanish-speaking Mexicans.

Mexico knew it was impossible to stop the flood of Americans into their land. Austin's scheme at least gave them some control. So they agreed to it. Each American family moving to Texas would get free land. But they had to give up their American citizenship and become Mexican citizens. If they did, they got to live tax-free for 10 years. On his way home from making the deal for Texas, Moses Austin got sick and died. On his deathbed he begged his son Stephen to go to Texas for him.

Who better to watch these guys? I have the fangs. I have the claws. What could happen?

Everything's Big in Texas —
Even the Bugs

Stephen Austin got to handpick the first 300 American families to go to Texas. (In Texas, they're known as the Old Three Hundred, like the First Families of Virginia, or New England's *Mayflower* descendants.) Austin took these families to the rich

Stephen Austin (1793–1836)

Stephen Austin, known as the Father of Texas, wasn't really wild. He was short, well educated, and refined. He had been born in Virginia, raised in Missouri, spent four years at Yale College when he was just a young teenager, and then graduated with distinction from Transylvania University in Kentucky. He spent his twenties as a businessman in Missouri, not exactly doing anything much of distinction. He loved music, dancing, and people with good manners. He didn't particularly want to go to Texas, but he

Texas land between the Brazos and Colorado rivers, near where the city of Austin is today. He promised them heaven on earth. That's not what they found.

The settlers did find good soil. Americans who moved to Texas bragged that the soil grew pumpkins so big that only a strong man could pull them

In Steve Austin's Texas

had made his father a deathbed promise and he kept it. He never married, and he later claimed that Texas was his bride. And he turned out to be a skillful diplomat, at first working well with the Mexican authorities. When he took the first group of Americans to Texas, Austin tried to make strict rules: no drinking or unsavory types wanted. Austin's rules didn't last, but he did get the state's capital named for him.

out of the ground. They said that everything was big in Texas, even the bullfrogs were as big as a man's head. Those were the good things. But there were a lot of bad big things, too, like the weather. People wrote back home that it was either blazing hot or freezing. On cold nights you could expect a rattlesnake to join you in bed. Even the insects were Texas-sized. There were seven-inch centipedes and quarter-pound tarantulas.

Life Was Not a Bowl of Cherries

The new immigrants to Texas became Mexican citizens, but they stuck together. Spanish art, poetry, music, and religion were all very important to most Mexicans. Most of the Americans never bothered to learn Spanish. Although they were supposed to have become Roman Catholics, few really did, or did so in name only. Many even made fun of the Catholic religion.

The early settlers had to clear the land, build a home from scratch, and put crops in. Most homes

'Course Texas is a part of Mexico. 'Course I'm a Mexican. What? Don't I look Mexican? Here . . . watch me talk some Mexican. Adios.

were two-room log cabins, with stick-and-mud chimneys for cooking. The cabins were windowless with dirt floors. Women worked harder than the men, who could at least take a little time out for hunting. One of the pioneers, Noah Smithwick, wrote, "Texas was heaven for men and dogs, hell for women and oxen." He might have included that it was hell for slaves, too.

Very shortly after Stephen Austin moved his first 300 families to Texas, all sorts of Americans

Slavery and Texas

If life was hard for the original white Americans in Texas, it was doubly hard on the slaves. Many of the settlers from the United States came with their slaves, even though slavery was officially illegal in Mexico. Mexico was far ahead of the United States in forbidding slavery. It was one of the first things Mexicans did when their country became a republic. In 1828, a new Mexican constitution said once again that slavery was illegal throughout the country, which, of course, meant Texas, too. In Texas, there was a momentary panic. Austin got the Mexican governors in Texas to create a paper fiction called "contract labor," which allowed the Americans to hold their slaves for 99 years or until death. Guess which usually came first? Children born to slaves were supposed to go free when they turned 14, but that rarely happened. By 1830, there were about 1,000 slaves in eastern Texas, where the Americans had settled.

decided to cross the border and get themselves some free land. The same economic bad times that had sent people to Oregon sent them to Texas. And Texas was much closer. Thousands of people scrawled "GTT" (gone to Texas) on their doors and

Jim Bowie (1796–1836) and His Knife

Jim Bowie grew up in Louisiana, claiming that he could ride the back of an alligator. He and his elder brother, Rezin, got rich smuggling slaves. There are a lot of legends about Jim Bowie, and it's hard to separate out the legends from the facts. There are even a lot of arguments about who designed the famous knife named after him. Some say it was his brother. Others say that Jim Bowie himself took a whittled design of the knife he wanted to James Black's blacksmith shop in Arkansas. The knife, pronounced **boo**-wie, is an extra-long knife with the back edge curved to a point and sharpened to a razor's edge. In 1827, near Natchez, Mississippi, Jim got into a bloody brawl and killed three men

headed west. They weren't Stephen Austin's refined folks, either. A lot of them were not the type you'd want to meet in a dark alley, or even a well-lit alley.

with his knife. Bowie had to get out of town. He moved to Texas. Bowie became a Mexican citizen, converted to Catholicism, and started a bunch of get-rich-quick schemes. He married the beautiful daughter of a wealthy Mexican vice-governor. In 1833, his wife and two children died of cholera. From then on, he made it his business to either fight for Texas independence from Mexico or die. He got to do both. (See pages 103–109.)

Shhh! Maybe if we're really, really quiet, they'll all just go away.

It's Hard to Uninvite Someone

In 1830, Mexico tried to slam the door shut. It said no more Americans would be allowed in. Fat chance. Mexico didn't have enough soldiers to patrol the border, and more and more Americans snuck in as illegal immigrants. Soon, eastern Texas had nearly 30,000 Anglo-Americans, nearly six times the Hispanic total. Rebellion was in the air and now it had a new leader, Sam Houston, one of the wildest of the wild bunch.

Texas Rebels

In 1833, Americans in Texas wanted to make Texas an independent state within Mexico. They sent Stephen Austin to Mexico City to tell the Mexican government. When Austin got there,

Sam Houston (1793–1863)

Sam Houston, born in Virginia, seemed to have been born restless. As a kid, he ran away from home. He lived with a Cherokee tribe in Tennessee that eventually adopted him. He said it was the best three years of his life. When Houston was a little older, he studied law and went into politics, but he never forgot his Cherokee friends. In Congress, he fought for Cherokee rights. He even dressed up in a Cherokee blanket and turban, as a sign of respect. His fellow white congressmen thought Houston was a hothead and a crazy man. He never seemed to tire of changing his outfit. He wore furry vests. He was the first man to wear beads in the U.S. Senate. He later became governor of Tennessee.

In 1829, his young wife left him. Houston gave up being governor. He began to drink heavily and his career seemed over. Houston headed home to the Cherokee. While he was with them, he said, "An eagle soared over my head — a great destiny waited for me in the West." Houston headed for Texas. A great destiny did await him, and soon a great city would have his name.

Mexico was undergoing yet another change of government. Ever since the Mexican revolution, one general after another had taken power. Now General Antonio López de Santa Anna was elected president of Mexico. Santa Anna didn't like rebellion, unless it was his. He threw Stephen Austin in jail and had himself declared dictator in 1834.

Come and Take It

In 1831, Mexico had given a cannon to the town of Gonzales, just west of present-day San Antonio. The cannon was supposed to protect the townspeople from raids by the Comanche. By 1835, Mexico was worried that the Texas rebels would use that cannon against Mexican troops. Santa Anna sent his brother-in-law to retrieve the cannon. The Americans in Gonzales wanted to keep it. Mrs. Naomi Dewitt even embroidered the words "Come and Take It" on her white silk wedding dress. The Texas rebels filled the cannon with horseshoes and shrapnel. As the sun came up on October 2, 1835, they fired the cannon directly at the Mexican army. One Mexican was killed, the rest retreated.

The Alamo Gang

Now Santa Anna really wanted to teach those Texas rebels a lesson. He raised an army of 5,000 and marched on Texas. He was sure he could wipe out those rebels lickety-split. Meanwhile, Santa Anna's wife convinced her husband to release Stephen Austin from prison. Once he got home, Austin was convinced that independence was the only way to go. He issued a call for Americans from Tennessee and Kentucky to come to Texas and help fight.

Sam Houston was named commander in chief of the Texas rebels. The problem was that Sam Houston didn't really have any organized troops. All he had was a bunch of volunteers, including many Mexicans who lived in Texas and hated Santa Anna. Nobody wanted to follow orders. For example, without orders from Houston, one group of volunteers marched into San Antonio and took over the old Mission of San Antonio de Valera, known as the Alamo.

It was quite a crowd in the Alamo. Jim Bowie was there, but he was drunk most of the time. There was William Barret Travis, a young lawyer from Alabama, who was a hothead, sure that independence could be won with a snap of his fingers. Then Davy Crockett from Tennessee showed up to help fight. He was even more famous than Jim Bowie and Sam Houston put together!

Remember the Alamo: Just Don't Forget That the Americans Lost

Fewer than two hundred rebels inside the Alamo. More than two thousand Mexican soldiers

Antonio López de Santa Anna (1794–1876), or How to Chew Gum and Be a General at the Same Time

Santa Anna loved power. "Were I made God," he said, "I should wish to be something more." Since the position of God was taken, Santa Anna declared himself the Napoleon of the West. He became a soldier at 16 and was a general before he was 26. He was totally ruthless and cared nothing for his soldiers' lives or anyone else's for that matter. He wore a sword worth $7,000.

Whenever Santa Anna went to war, which was quite often, he did so with a silk tent, wine bottles with gold stoppers, crates of champagne, boxes of chocolate, and a silver chamber pot. Santa Anna kept coming into and going out of power. Around 1866, he spent a year in exile in Staten Island, New York. On Staten Island, he needed a secretary, so he hired a man named Thomas Adams. Adams noticed that the general liked to chew on pieces of a plant from Mexico called *chicle*. When

Santa Anna left New York to go back to Mexico, he gave Adams some chicle. Adams experimented with it, using different flavors like peppermint and spearmint. He called it "New York's #1 Gum, Snapping and Stretching." Ever since then, teachers have been trying to get American kids to stop chewing gum in school.

> They say I, General Santa Anna, don't care about my soldiers. I love my soldiers! They're so comfortable!

outside. It was never going to be a fair fight. Santa Anna never intended it to be. *"En esta guerra no habrá prisioneros"* ("In this war there will be no prisoners"), he declared. Santa Anna sent up a bloodred flag that meant "surrender or die."

On March 6, 1836, at 5:00 A.M., Santa Anna gave orders to play "El Degüello" or "the throat slitting." It is the music that is still played in the bullring today to signal that it is the end — either the matador or the bull will die. Twice the Mexican army charged, and twice the American Texans kept them from coming over the walls. On the third charge, Colonel Travis was shot through the head.

Once the Mexicans were over the wall, there was no hope for the rebels. Joe, Travis's black slave, claimed that Jim Bowie fought from his sickbed. Nobody knows if that is true or not. Some say Davy

They're playing "El Degüello," the some-body's-going-to-cash-it-in song. Okay, enough with the head-smashing stuff. I'm going to samurai all over this guy.

Davy Crockett (1786–1836)

Davy Crockett never walked away from a good fight. When he was about 10, he got in a fight with a bully and never really went back to school. He taught himself to read and write, and, most important of all, he taught himself to shoot a rifle. He wound up getting involved first in local Tennessee politics, and then in 1827, he got elected to Congress. Crockett was smart, but he was also a smart aleck. He loved to make fun of himself, and nobody could tell when he was making up a tall tale or telling the truth. "I'm Davy Crockett," he'd say. "Fresh from the backwoods, half horse, half alligator, a little touched with the snapping turtle. . . . I can whip my weight in wildcats and hug a bear too close for comfort." Everyone called him Davy, and soon Davy was one of the most famous men in Congress. In 1833, he lost his Congressional seat, and in 1835, Crockett decided to go to Texas. He eventually arrived at the Alamo with about a dozen top-notch shots from Tennessee.

Crockett killed seven Mexican soldiers at the end, battling them with his rifle, Betsy. Others say that Crockett was captured alive, tortured, and then killed. It cost Santa Anna 600 of his men to kill the 189 rebels. Santa Anna ordered that the rebels' bodies be doused with oil and burned. Ever since ancient times, burning your dead enemies instead of burying them has been considered the worst insult.

How Do You Write History When Almost Everyone Who Was There Dies?

What really happened at the Alamo during the 13 days it was under siege from February 23 to March 6, 1836? There were at least 13 survivors, including several women and children, and at least a few men. But their stories often changed over the years. For example, Travis's slave, Joe, escaped and said that after Travis was shot, with his dying breath he plunged his sword into the Mexican General Ventura Mora and killed him. The only trouble with that story is that Mora didn't die until 1853, which was nearly twenty years later.

Many of the most famous details of what went on at the Alamo just before the last battle came from Lewis Rose, who said he was one of the last to escape. Rose claimed that Travis drew a line in the sand with his sword and said, "All who are willing to die with me, cross this line." Jim Bowie had men carry him across in his cot. Rose wrote, "I stole a glance at Colonel Bowie in his cot. Colonel Davy Crockett was leaning over, talking to him. After a few seconds, Bowie looked at me and said, 'You don't seem willing to die with us, Rose.' 'No,' I said. 'I am not. . . .' Then I sprang up, seized my traveling bed and unwashed clothes. Standing on the top [of the wall], I glanced down to take a last look at my friends . . . overpowered by my feelings, I turned away." Rose went over the wall and escaped. The only problem is that Rose didn't write his story down until almost 20 years later and he was known as a guy who lied a lot.

TRAVEL

The Alamo in downtown San Antonio, Texas, has been restored and is one of the most visited historic sites in the nation. There are walking tours and guides to take you through the events, and in late February and early March, the Battle of the Alamo is re-created.

If You Think the Alamo Was Bad, Read About Goliad

It looked as if Santa Anna would quickly snuff out the Texas Revolution. After the Alamo, he marched east into rebel territory. Four hundred American rebels were trapped by part of Santa Anna's army near Goliad. They surrendered. Santa Anna ordered all of the unarmed men shot. Even his own generals and many of his troops were horrified. The wife of a Mexican officer, Señora Francita Alavez, hid several wounded rebels under her bed and helped them escape. She became known as the Angel of Goliad. Other Mexican soldiers, ashamed of what

Sure, ordering hundreds of unarmed soldiers shot makes me look like not such a nice guy. But look at it from my side: I was trying . . there was a . . . Okay, you got me. I'm not such a nice guy.

their general was ordering them to do, hid prisoners in their own beds, covering them with their bodies during the slaughter. Out of 407 American rebels, only 48 survived.

Santa Anna was determined to terrorize all the American settlers into leaving Texas. He gave orders to burn every American town, home, farm, and ranch. Thousands of Americans ran home to Louisiana. Everybody wanted Sam Houston to fight the Mexican army, but Houston knew that he was outnumbered. He kept his small army in full retreat, zigzagging across Texas. Rumors flew that Houston was drunk. Settlers jeered at him from the sidelines. Houston just chewed on raw corn and read Julius Caesar's memoirs (in the original Latin), which he kept in his saddlebag.

Santa Anna's troops followed Houston into the swamplands around the San Jacinto River, a few miles from the present-day city of Houston. Santa Anna thought he had the American rebels trapped and outnumbered. April 21, 1836, was a Thursday. It was a hot, muggy day, and Santa Anna decided it would be safe to take a siesta. He went into his silk tent and told his men they could take a rest, too. Just a little ways away, Sam Houston told his troops that it was going to be a good day to fight a battle (actually he used a mild cuss word, so we won't use a direct quote). Houston was ready to make a stand.

The Yellow Rose of Texas

Santa Anna loved the ladies, and even in battle he didn't like to be alone. He stole Emily, a slave girl, from a Texas settler and rebel, Colonel James Morgan. On the afternoon of the battle, Emily kept Santa Anna busy as they drank champagne. Santa Anna was so involved with Emily that when the battle cries filled the air, he did nothing to rally his troops. In fact, he barely escaped in his underwear and red slippers. Emily's story became a famous legend, and the song "The Yellow Rose of Texas" was written about her.

Caught with His Pants Down

Sam Houston gathered his men together. He ordered them to line up and said, "Trust in God and fear not. Remember Goliad. Remember the Alamo!" Houston led the charge riding his horse, Saracen. Five slugs hit Saracen and he was killed. Houston switched to another horse. This one was killed, too. A musket ball splintered Houston's right leg, but he kept fighting. The battle lasted just 18 minutes. The Mexicans surrendered, but the slaughter went on for another hour. The rebels took their revenge for Goliad. Around 600 Mexican soldiers died, compared to just 6 of the rebels. Santa Anna escaped from his tent. He was found running away, wearing muddy long johns. He tried to pretend that he was just a private. His lies didn't work, especially when he was dragged back, and his men stood up shouting, *"El presidente, el presidente. . . ."*

Santa Anna was taken to see Sam Houston. Houston was sitting on a blanket under an oak tree, recovering from his leg wound. Santa Anna pleaded for his life. Houston's men wanted to kill Santa Anna and skin him, but Houston knew Santa Anna was more valuable to him alive than dead. He made Santa Anna sign a treaty giving Texas its independence. Then Texas adopted a brand-new flag: red, white, and blue with a lone star. So now there were three republics in the West: the Republic of Texas, the Republic of Mexico, and the United States.

San Jacinto Museum and Battlefield Monument, San Jacinto, Texas. Built 100 years after the battle it honors, the 570-foot San Jacinto Monument stands in the *Guinness Book of World Records* as the tallest monument column in the world. It towers over the prairie where, in 1836, General Sam Houston and his determined army battled furiously to the cries of "Remember the Alamo!"

I always wondered

why I was supposed to remember the Alamo. Ever since I can, well, "remember," people have been telling me to "Remember the Alamo!" I didn't even know what the Alamo was, let alone why I should remember it. Yet I was so familiar with the phrase "Remember the Alamo!" that I was always afraid I actually knew exactly what it was, but, for some reason, I forgot. How could I *forget* the Alamo?! Especially with so many people constantly reminding me to

remember it. It really bugged me. Which is a weird thing to say: that something "bugged" me. Especially considering that *I'm* a bug. That would imply that I don't like myself, but that's not true. I'm a very friendly bug who would never bug anybody. I mean "bother" anybody. I didn't mean to say "bug."

Anyway . . . what was I talking about?

Oh, right! The Alamo. I almost forgot. Now *that* would have bugged me.

Chapter 5

War! Not So Glorious!

Santa Anna's political career went down the toilet after he lost Texas. He had to go into exile. Mexico didn't accept that Texas was independent. They wanted it back. Meanwhile, Sam Houston wanted Texas to become a part of the United States. Texas applied to become a state. Congress refused at first. Northerners argued that Texas would upset the balance between free states and slave states.

While Congress argued, ordinary American

TIME LINE

1842
John C. Frémont explores California

1845
United States annexes Texas

1846
Congress declares war on Mexico; Donner Party tries to reach California; Bear Flag Republic in California

116

It's not that I don't appreciate everything you've done. I just need to get out on my own. You need to let me grow up, see other countries.

citizens took the law into their own hands, illegally moving into Texas and even farther west into what was clearly Mexican territory — California. Politicians and newspaper editors began proclaiming that America had a "manifest destiny" to stretch from sea to sea. On March 1, 1845, Texas was invited to become a state, just three days before a new president, James Polk, was inaugurated. Polk definitely believed in "manifest destiny."

1848
Mexico signs treaty
giving up California
and New Mexico

President James K. Polk (1795–1849)

James Polk was born in North Carolina, and elected president in 1844. He campaigned saying that the United States should stretch from the Atlantic to the Pacific oceans. He wanted Texas to become a state, and he wanted to take over California, too.

Polk's wife, Sarah, managed his affairs and was known for her charm and intelligence, something Polk wasn't famous for. Even those who voted for Polk considered him humorless and rigid. He complained about visiting groups of schoolchildren and tourists staring at him while he ate. He banned dancing and liquor in the White House. But as soon as he took office, he went to work trying to stretch America's borders.

California, Here We Come

California was so far from Mexico City that the few Mexicans who lived there felt lonely. In the beginning, they didn't mind that people from other nations came to live and trade with them. Immigrants from many different countries, including Russia, Switzerland, and Germany, as well as Americans, chose to settle in California and take Mexican citizenship.

John C. Frémont's journals influenced many Americans' decisions to go to California. The route was much less sure and much more dangerous than the well-traveled Oregon Trail.

More! More! More! War!

The new state of Texas claimed that its territory stretched all the way to the Rio Grande, while the Mexican government thought it ended at the Nueces River. President Polk sent a negotiator to Mexico City to try to settle the matter. President Polk offered to buy California and New Mexico.

Mexico was insulted. How would the United States have felt if Mexico had offered to buy half of *its* country? Mexican newspapers demanded war against the *Bárbaros de Norte* (Barbarians of the North) and revenge for San Jacinto.

Meanwhile, back in the United States, President Polk and members of his Democratic party were ready for war. The United States would take over California and fulfill America's destiny to stretch from sea to sea. Newspapers in New York City said it would be a "short and glorious war, an adventure full of fun and frolic." Some newspapers even called for the United States to take over all of Mexico.

Jessie Frémont (1824–1902) and John C. Frémont (1813–1890)

Jessie Frémont was born Jessie Benton, the daughter of powerful Senator Thomas Hart Benton from Missouri. Senator Benton was a big supporter of the idea that America's destiny was to expand. His beautiful daughter thought so, too. But Daddy wasn't very happy when 17-year-old Jessie eloped with an adventurer, John C. Frémont, on October 19, 1841. Jessie eventually persuaded her father to help John get a job scouting the West for the government. Frémont had the good sense to hire Kit Carson as a guide, and they ended up traveling all the way to California. When her husband returned, Jessie took his journals and whipped them into shape. She was a talented writer and editor. Frémont's journals of the West became best-sellers. Frémont was hailed as a national hero and nicknamed the Pathfinder, even though Kit Carson had done most of the pathfinding.

Behind the scenes there was a lot going on. President Polk was negotiating with the deposed leader of the Mexican army, Santa Anna. He thought if he could get Santa Anna back in charge of the Mexican army, together they could reach a peace that would leave the United States with huge portions of Mexican territory and limited casualties.

The Bugs Go Crazy

President Polk sent General Zachary Taylor down to the edge of the Rio Grande in Corpus Christi, Texas, then a tiny town of less than 100 people. Suddenly, Corpus Christi had to cope with 4,000 American troops. The soldiers put up their tents. The rains came, and the tents leaked. This was Texas, home of the big bugs. There were scorpions, centipedes, and tarantulas. Lice got into everyone's clothing. Then there were the ants . . .

Okay. They have 4,000 guys. We can still win, but we have to be organized. Lice: keep thinking "hair." Centipedes: wiggle out from under stuff, that really scares 'em! Beetles: lay your eggs in their food. Scorpions: go for their shoes. Everybody stay focused. Good luck!

The Donner Dinner Party (Skip If You Don't Like Unappetizing Meals)

In 1846, the families of George and Jacob Donner and James Frazier Reed and others went by wagon to make a new life for themselves in the valley of California. Everything went fine until they reached Wyoming. Then they met a guide who promised them he knew a shortcut through the desert. Some shortcut. They ended up stuck in the desert, with their oxen dying and running away from them. They had to carry what little they could out of the desert into the mountains near what is now Lake Tahoe. Snow is great for skiers, but it's awful if you're not prepared for it. The first heavy snows fell on the Donner Party on October 30, 1846. And the bad weather never let up. Six weeks later, they faced the fact that unless someone rescued them, they were trapped until spring. They killed and ate all of their cattle, boiled the hides and chewed on them. They even killed their dog, "eating his head and feet and hide and everything about him." Then, dying parents began begging their children to have them for dinner. At first the survivors refused, but then after going three days without any food, they ate the bodies of the dead, carefully wrapping up pieces of limbs so that nobody had to knowingly eat their own relatives. Survivor Virginia Reed, just 13 during the ordeal, wrote to her cousin after her rescue, "Oh Mary, don't let this letter dishaten [dishearten] anybody and never take no cutoffs and hury [hurry] along as fast as you can."

armies of them. "Last night," a soldier joked in a letter, "the ants tried to carry me off in my sleep."

Army food didn't make life in camp any easier. The daily ration was beans and a little pickled food. The biscuits were full of beetle grubs.

The drinking water was polluted, and the men stank. Disease spread throughout the camp. In fact, all through the Mexican War, disease killed far more soldiers than gunfire. The soldiers complained about it all, but the enlisted men had one thing going for them. Their general shared their hardships with them. They loved their general, "Old Zach."

The War Begins

Old Zach positioned his troops on the disputed border of the Rio Grande. The Mexican army was on the other side. On April 4, 1846, the two armies stood across the river, each one spoiling for a fight. From Mexico's point of view, Taylor's army was on their land. The president of Mexico ordered an attack on April 24, 1846. The Mexican cavalry, 1,600 men strong, crossed the river on horseback.

Taylor sent a 60-man patrol to keep track of the cavalry. The patrol was surrounded and either captured or killed. Taylor sent word by steamboat and then by mounted courier to President Polk: "American blood has been shed on American soil." The truth was that the soil was the disputed land between Mexico and Texas. But Polk used Taylor's

words to spur Congress to declare war on Mexico. Now it was official! It was war!

New Mexico Falls

Now that war was declared, all of Mexico's lands were up for grabs. General Stephen Watts Kearny, of Fort Leavenworth, Kansas, organized what is now called the Army of the West. This band of volunteers, enlisted men, and Mormons (Brigham Young thought offering troops to the Army would be a convenient way to get the U.S. government on his side) managed to take all of New Mexico. The few Mexican settlers in New Mexico had been abused and ignored by the Mexican government for years. They didn't see how being part of the United States could be any worse.

General Zachary "Old Rough and Ready" Taylor (1784–1850)

General Zachary Taylor didn't look like a general. He didn't like to wear a uniform unless he had to. He much preferred straw hats, baggy pants, and dusty coats. When he sat on his favorite horse, Old Whitey, Taylor slumped in the saddle and chewed tobacco. He "looks like a toad," complained a West Point military man. But most of the men who fought with Zachary Taylor loved him. They called him Old Zach or Old Rough and Ready because he wasn't a spit-and-polish kind of guy. Taylor didn't keep guards around his tent, so anyone could drop in. He almost always took time to listen to soldiers' complaints. Taylor became so famous after the Mexican War that he went on to become president of the United States in 1849.

The Antiwar Movement

Not all Americans supported this war. After all, Texas *had* belonged to Mexico. California and New Mexico certainly were still legally part of Mexico. Ulysses S. Grant, who fought in the Mexican War, later called it "one of the most unjust [wars] ever waged by a stronger nation against a weaker nation." Americans who hated slavery were almost all against the war because they thought that the South wanted the war as a way of spreading slavery into Mexican territory. Frederick Douglass, himself an escaped slave, wrote that the war made him "sick at heart." In Massachusetts, the noted writer Henry David Thoreau refused to pay his taxes because the money went toward the war; he went to jail for a night before his friends bailed him out.

David and Goliath: a great story, but apparently not the greatest plan at all times.

Almost all of what are today the states of New Mexico, Arizona, Utah, Nevada, and southern Colorado fell to General Kearny's army at the beginning of the war.

California: A Bear
of a Republic for One Month

In California, nobody yet knew that America was at war with Mexico. In December of 1845, John C. Frémont returned to California with more than 60 armed men. With no authority whatsoever, he and his gang seized Sutter's Fort (near present-day Sacramento). On June 14, 1846, General Mariano Vallejo, one of the wealthiest Mexicans in the valley, surrendered to Frémont in Sonoma. Frémont and his men drank Vallejo's brandy and announced that they were setting up an independent republic. They hoisted up a sheet with a rough drawing of a grizzly bear on it (some people said it looked more like a hog). "A band of horse thieves and runaway sailors," Vallejo wrote his wife. The Bear State Republic lasted all of about a month.

Meanwhile, U.S. naval ships had seized all the key ports in California and raised the American flag above customhouses in San Francisco and Monterey. Then Kearny and his men marched from New Mexico into California. That's when Frémont went too far. He refused to take orders from General Kearny, his superior. Frémont eventually faced charges of mutiny and was court-martialed and forced to leave the army. The Bear Flag was taken down and the Stars and Stripes flew in its place.

To the Halls of Montezuma

So far, the war had been going well for the United States. They had taken over New Mexico and California. President Polk had gotten what he wanted. But the United States couldn't really keep those territories in the eyes of the law unless Mexico signed a treaty, admitting they had lost. The problem was that Mexico wouldn't give in.

Polk planned to pay to get Santa Anna back in charge of the Mexican army. This turned into a disaster. Once he was back in Mexico and in charge,

Give up yet?

Not yet.

Now?

Don't think so.

Soon?

Maybe.

Por favor!

Santa Anna broke his promises to Polk, organized a huge army, and got himself declared president of Mexico.

If the United States wanted a treaty, they would have to march into Mexico itself. The soldiers with Old Rough and Ready were ordered to attack from the north. Taylor's troops were sick and they had very few supplies. Still, Taylor marched into the desert lands of what is now northern Mexico. His soldiers were dying from the heat and from cholera. "The death march was ever in our ears," Lieutenant George B. McClellan wrote. "They died like dogs." Mockingbirds learned the death march, the bugle song played over a soldier's dead body. One out of eight American soldiers died of illness in just a few weeks (as many as would die in battles during the entire war). The death march through northern Mexico convinced the United States that they never could take Mexico by land.

Back in Washington, General Winfield Scott suggested to President Polk that they take Mexico by sea. At six feet four inches tall and weighing 240 pounds, General Scott was everything that Old Rough and Ready wasn't. He loved uniforms. Scott directed the largest amphibious landing in history. More than 12,000 mostly seasick American troops landed at Vera Cruz, Mexico. From there they marched inland toward Mexico City. They followed the same route that Cortés had used to conquer Montezuma, the Aztec ruler, in 1519.

It turned into brutal, ruthless war on both sides. General Scott wrote that his troops had "committed atrocities to make Heaven weep and every American of Christian morals blush for the country."

Finally, the U.S. Marines raised the American flag over the National Palace in Mexico City. Whenever the Marines sing about marching from the "halls of Montezuma," they are singing about the Mexican War. Mexico City is where Montezuma once ruled the mighty Aztec empire. Santa Anna was forced to resign and Mexico finally agreed to work out a treaty with the United States.

The End of the War

The war hadn't come cheap to either the United States or Mexico. It claimed the lives of more than 13,000 Americans, most of them soldiers

Sure, it's embarrassing for the great General Santa Anna to surrender twice. But on the upside: at least I'm wearing my pants this time!

Día de Los Niños Heroes de Chapultepec

In September of 1847, more than 100 teenage Mexican cadets refused to leave a castle just outside Mexico City's walls. Ordered to retreat, they still insisted on fighting for their nation. September 14 is still celebrated in Mexico as the Day of the Boy Heroes of Chapultepec.

who died of disease, and probably about 20,000 Mexicans, who died in battles or from disease.

Mexico and the United States signed the Treaty of Guadalupe-Hidalgo on February 2, 1848. Mexico agreed to give up all claim to Texas and made the Rio Grande the international border. It also gave up all of New Mexico and California. The United States agreed to pay Mexico $15,000,000 for this territory.

Lucky for the Americans that news traveled slowly in those days. Mexico had thought they were giving away mostly useless territory. About the same time that the treaty was signed, something big was happening in California that would change everything.

America finally

stretched from sea to shining sea. I guess all that was left was to figure out how people could get from one end of the country to the other without having to eat each other! Too bad the Donner Party didn't discover a Mickey D's along the way.

OREGON TRAIL

Things sure are moving along for America, though, aren't they? We started off with just 13 states and now we have enough land for 35 more. If my math is correct, that's, like . . . twice as many states . . . I think. (I was never very good at math.)

SUTTER'S FORT

By the way, I thought you might be interested to know that I'm actually half Mexican. My mother was born there and everybody knew her as La Cucaracha. That's Spanish for "the cockroach." My mother is famous. There's even a Spanish song about her. Maybe I'll teach it to you sometime. Right now, though, I want to find out what was going on in California that was such a big deal.

LOUISIANA
PURCHASE

THE
ALAMO

Chapter 6
Seeing the Elephant! (Maybe)

"**G**old, gold, gold, from the American River!" shouted Sam Brannan as he strutted up and down the main streets of San Francisco, California. Sam was a Mormon shopkeeper. He held a glass vial filled with gold dust in his hand, gold sifted from the bed of the American River at the foothills of the Sierra Nevada. In a few days, almost the entire population of San Francisco was on its way to the mountains, looking to strike it rich.

TIME LINE

January 24, 1848
Gold discovered at Sutter's Mill

June 14, 1848
San Francisco half empty

1849
California's population soars

We're Off to See the Elephant!

So many people rushed to find gold that they had their own music and their own jargon. One popular song was called "Seeing the Elephant." It came from an old story about a farmer who heard there was a circus in town. He had never seen an elephant so he hooked up his horse to a wagon and filled it with vegetables to sell at the market in the town where the circus was playing. The circus was having a parade, led by an elephant. The farmer's horse got so spooked that it bolted and

Are you okay, honey?

Sure, I'm just getting a really, really good look at this here elephant.

overturned the wagon. The farmer lost all his vegetables. "Aren't you sorry?" asked the farmer's friends. "I don't give a hang," the farmer said. "At least I have seen the elephant."

People headed west saying they were "going to see the elephant." And when they came back without getting rich, they said, "Well, at least I've seen the elephant" (or maybe just the elephant's tail, meaning they had an adventure and got to see California).

Hitting Pay Dirt

The gold rush started on January 24, 1848. James Marshall (not the children's-book writer) was overseeing the construction of a sawmill at Sutter's Mill, near present-day Sacramento. Marshall spotted something shiny in the riverbed. He took it to his boss, Captain John Sutter. They tested it every way they knew, hammering it, dropping it in a pot of lye, biting it, etc. Finally, they were pretty sure what they had found was . . . gold! They wanted to keep it secret, but humans are funny. They just can't keep a secret, especially about something as exciting as gold.

The gold that James Marshall discovered in the American River was part of a deposit that runs for several hundred miles up and down the Sierra Nevada. Gold, like other minerals, is formed deep inside the earth. Deposits, or veins, of gold are usually found inside quartz. Usually it's very hard to

Some Terrible Secret Keepers of History

get to. But gold is heavier than quartz and the other surrounding minerals. As the water of a river washes away other minerals, the heavier gold is left behind. In California, the water had washed away the quartz and gold came loose and trickled into the water in the form of dust, flakes, and chunky nuggets.

"I Got a Violent Attack of Gold Fever"

At first, the gold really was just lying in the streams. One man found $9,000 worth of gold in just one afternoon. News of the California gold

Have You Ever Wondered Why Gold Is So Valuable?

Gold is one of the most precious substances on earth. First of all, there is not very much of it. You could fit all the gold in the world (125,000 tons) on one large freight ship. In 1848, there was even less gold around. All the known gold in the entire world in 1848 could have fit in a large classroom.

Gold does not decay, rust, or age in any way. The gold that ancient peoples used to make coins and jewelry still shines like it did thousands of years ago. Gold is extremely dense but very flexible. You could stretch an ounce of gold (an amount you can hold in the palm of your hand) into a 50-mile-long wire.

Gold became a form of money in many parts of the ancient world. It was pressed into coins that were used in trading. Gold became the symbol of wealth in the world. It is still considered very valuable.

strikes spread across the United States and across the world. Men and women from New York to New Zealand began calling their unstoppable urge to travel to California "gold fever." One man described the symptoms in a newspaper article: "A frenzy seized my soul. Piles of gold rose up before me at every step; castles of marble. . . . In short, I had a very violent attack of Gold Fever."

Oh, yeah! Woooo!!! I've struck pizza! Yeaaahhh!

I wonder: if you love pizza way more than you love gold, would that be "pizza fever"?

Arg! I'm an Argonaut!

The first gold seekers to reach California from the East Coast were those who took a dangerous and expensive sea journey. These adventurers were called Argonauts, after the mythical ancient Greek seamen who had traveled with Jason on the ship the *Argo* in search of the Golden Fleece.

If you were traveling to California by sea in 1849, you had two choices. You could travel all the way around the southern tip of South America, called Cape Horn, and back up the other side to California, or you could try a shortcut. The shortcut, now the country of Panama, was often just called the Isthmus, which is Greek for "neck, or narrow passage." Panama is the thinnest piece of land between the Atlantic and Pacific oceans.

Argonauts traveled to Panama and then made a dangerous riverboat and mule journey across the country. They hoped to find room on a boat on the Pacific side, cutting their sea voyage in half. They often had to wait months in disease-ridden seaside towns before a boat with room on board arrived. Some Argonauts got this far, turned around, and went home.

Meanwhile, the Argonauts who headed around Cape Horn had to suffer through horrible storms and many months at sea. But at least they didn't have to catch more than one boat!

The Argonauts weren't the only ones who had caught gold fever. The sailors who brought them to California often caught it, too. It was very common for the entire crew to abandon ship as soon as they reached the San Francisco harbor. Pleading captains and promises of extra pay were not enough to keep the men from jumping ship and heading for the mines. U.S. Navy ships had to put out to sea to try to stop their sailors from deserting.

The harbor had so many abandoned ships in it that the masts looked like a floating forest. Some opportunistic settlers took advantage of all the floating real estate and lived on the ships. Why sleep in a tent in the rain when you could sleep in a cozy cabin?

Forty-niners: Going for Gold, Not the Superbowl

Suddenly, there was bumper-to-bumper traffic on the Oregon Trail as thousands of Americans left home in 1849 and traveled overland to find gold. Sometimes there were 100 miles of wagons on the trail and fierce jockeying to get up front, ahead of the dust.

How the San Francisco 49ers Got Their Name

San Francisco's football team is named for all the people who rushed out to California in 1849. Between 50,000 and 80,000 people headed into California in just one year. A lot of them would have done just fine on the present-day football team because most of the gold rushers were young men with strong backs and strong arms. They needed to be strong because panning for gold was hard work. "A person thinking of coming to California ought to consider whether he can stand to work all day, under a hot sun, up to the knees in water and mud," wrote one forty-niner.

Conditions were much worse than in the earlier days of the Oregon Trail. The grasslands were so overgrazed that the forty-niners had to go miles off the trail to search for grass for their animals. The worst part was the stink. If the trail had stunk in the early days, imagine thousands of young men, each trying to get there ahead of each other, never changing their clothes. Unlike the families bound for Oregon before them, most of the forty-niners only planned to stay in the West long enough to make their fortunes. They hoped to return rich and triumphant to their homes back in the East.

Gold fever wasn't the only disease that the Argonauts and overlanders caught. Historians estimate that as much as 20 percent of gold rush travelers died of cholera during their trip or after they reached California.

I just heard two out of every ten prospectors is going to die. So I think the best thing for all of us is for a couple of you fellas to volunteer. C'mon now, let's not be selfish!

Gum San: **Land of Golden Mountain**

One of the first gold miners up near Sutter's Mill was Wong Chun Ming. He wrote home to China about striking it rich. Soon rumors spread in China that America was *Gum San,* the Land of the Golden Mountain. Ten years after the first gold strike in 1848, an estimated 35,000 Chinese had made the long journey to America to join the gold rush. Most came with the idea of striking it rich in America and then returning home.

At first, many Chinese wrote home that "California was a nice country without mandarins and soldiers." But within months, the new mining camps passed laws that forbade any foreigners or "other races" to live there. The Chinese were forced to mine areas where white American men wouldn't go because they were already picked over. They were only allowed to take jobs that white

Americans wouldn't touch, such as cook or laundryman. And if the Chinese did manage to make money (which a number of them did), they were in danger of being robbed or killed.

Life in Hangtown, Gouge Eye, Whiskeytown, Pokertown

All those tens of thousands of newcomers had to go somewhere. Up and down the gold-bearing rivers of northern California, towns popped up as often as prairie dogs on the plains. Folks had a great time naming these towns, often after the kind of life they were leading. They picked names like Hangtown, Gouge Eye, Whiskeytown, Pokertown, You Bet, and Rough and Ready.

Women in the Gold Rush

The ratio of men to women in the early days of the gold rush was nearly 12 to 1. Men sometimes would stand for hours just to see a woman. "I was never handsome in my best days," wrote Lucretia Wilson, who came out with her husband. She said that men came 40 miles just to see her. Her husband never found gold, but Lucretia found a way to strike it rich. She started an inn and fed as many as 300 boarders at a time. "A smart woman can do very well," she wrote. "Must work all the time — but plenty to do — and good pay."

Seems I'm having pretty good luck finding gold on these here prospector fellas, and that's a whole lot more comfy than sloshing around in a river looking for it.

At first, most gold miners lived in tents or just slept on the ground. After a while, some of them built huts made from green branches and canvas, or lean-tos made of whatever materials they could get. Slowly, houses and other wooden buildings began to appear around the diggings or streams. Most were very poorly made and the walls inside were actually made of paper. "It is just such a piece of carpentering as a child two years old, gifted with the strength of a man, would produce," wrote Mrs. Louisa Amelia Knapp Smith Clappe, who wrote letters that were published in newspapers back in the East under the name Dame Shirley. She also reported that she could hear almost any language you could imagine in those towns. In just one day, she heard Germans, Italians, Chileans, Hindus, Russians, and native Californians all trying to talk to one another.

Despair

The gold that was easy to find was soon gone, but the forty-niners kept coming. There was still gold in the riverbeds, but finding it became harder and harder. A typical miner spent 10 hours a day knee-deep in ice-cold water, digging, sifting, and washing. It was backbreaking labor that yielded fewer and fewer nuggets or flakes of gold. As panning became less effective, the miners moved to more advanced techniques, which often meant gouging out whole hillsides in order to get at the precious metal. But it wasn't just the hills that were being ruined.

As miners pushed out into the more remote territories searching for gold, they took over land that had belonged to the Chumash and other tribes. In 1848, there were about 150,000 Native Americans living in California. In 1870, there were probably only 31,000. Many Native Americans had died of diseases introduced by the settlers, but many were just plain murdered. Gold greed caused many white miners to shoot anybody who got in their way. White men could do this and not worry because laws were passed that forbade any Asians, Blacks, Native Americans, Mexicans, or South Americans to testify in court cases involving whites.

Mining the Miners, or Anyone Want to Pay $100 for a Glass of Water?

Many smart people soon realized that they could get much more gold out of the miners than they could out of the rivers. Some sharp business-men filled their wagons with barrels of water and went out in the deserts of Nevada charging the wagon trains trying to get to California as much as $100 for a bottle of water. Far more people got rich selling things to miners than ever got rich from gold. You're probably wearing one of those people's pants right now. Check out Levi Strauss on pages 148–149.

San Francisco Boomtown

Before the gold rush, San Francisco was a little mission town with just a few hundred people. By 1850, more than 20,000 people were living there. Sometimes as many as 30 houses would go up in one day.

When the newly rich miners came down from the hills to San Francisco, they wanted fun. They

Levi Strauss (1829?–1902)

Levi Strauss was a Jewish orphan who came to America from Germany. He and his uncles started a store in New York. He was about 20 years old when he arrived in San Francisco with some canvas that he hoped to sell for tents. A gruff old prospector chided young Strauss for not having brought along a supply of pants, because prospecting for gold was rough on pants. Strauss cut his canvas and stitched it into trousers. They were an instant success and became known as Levi's. He soon opened his own com-

found it. There were more than 500 bars in San Francisco. Entertainers, like Lola Montez (see pages 150–151), came from all over just to find ways to separate a miner from his gold. Samuel Clemens, who would later change his name to Mark Twain, was a young man during the gold rush. He wrote, "They were rough in those times. They fairly reveled in gold, whisky, fights, and fandangos."

pany, Levi Strauss & Co., on Battery Street in San Francisco. A few years later, Strauss switched from canvas to some blue denim cloth that he got in France. A lifelong bachelor, he left the company to four nephews, whose descendants still control it. Today, Levi's are sold around the world, with about $5 billion in annual sales.

It's rumored before Levi Strauss hit on his world-famous canvas pants, he toyed with a few less successful variations:

bologna   pinecone   Chihuahua

From Sea to Shining Sea . . .
Now What Do We Do?

When Lewis and Clark and the Corps of Discovery started their journey in 1804, there was no map of the West. By 1850, there were maps that

Lola Montez (1818–1861)

Lola Montez was actually born in Ireland as Marie Dolores Eliza Rosanna Gilbert. She wanted to become an actress, but she wasn't very good at acting, so she changed her name to Lola Montez and called herself a Spanish dancer. She wasn't very good at dancing, either. Montez was booed off the stage in London. But she stuck to it and drifted around Europe, meeting famous men. When Lola Montez heard about the gold rush, she knew she had to be there. She went to San Francisco by boat. On her opening

showed the trails, rivers, and roads that could take you from the Atlantic to the Pacific. Maps had been published in nearly every newspaper in the land. Anybody who wanted to could get a rough map. The West had become crisscrossed with wagon trails, and even regular stagecoaches and mail ser-

night, she charged $65 a ticket and did her Spanish dance. The critics thought she stank, but the audience loved her. Montez went on to open a frontier saloon in one of the mining camps, where she charged top prices. Her saloon was famous for her billiard table that had dragons carved on its legs.

Lola's grand San Francisco debut earns seven big thumbs down (and one plugged nose)!

vice. Moving out West was no longer a strange thing for weird mountain men to do. The West was becoming a place where ordinary people went to make a new start.

The gold rush and all those people from back East turned into a disaster for all of the western Native American tribes. At the beginning, most tribes found they could live with a few whites passing through their territory. They even liked trading with white people. But now there were hundreds of thousands of whites in their territory. Most of those white people thought that the Native American tribes were just in the way.

With the gold rush, the prairie lands became overgrazed. Soon other gold rushes would follow in Colorado and Montana. Native Americans would be forced to give up their lands. Eventually, they would be pushed so far that they would have no choice but to fight back.

The United States in 1850 had gone way beyond even Thomas Jefferson's great imagination. Its borders now extended from sea to shining sea. Many of the problems that the United States had had from the beginning — slavery, prejudice against outsiders, lawlessness — Americans took west with them. These problems would have to be dealt with soon. But in the meantime, a new myth had been born. It didn't have to do with any "American Monsters." There were no prehistoric monsters still roaming in the West. Americans began to think of themselves as adventurers and risk takers, as a people who long for a better life and aren't afraid to grab it. It is a dream that still lives on.

Howdy, fellow

prospector! It's sort of like I was made for this job, isn't it? I just knew that moving out West would pan out. Get it? "Pan" out? Well, the least you can do is laugh. I've been standing in this freezing-cold river since page one just so I could tell that joke!

Anyway, it sure didn't take long for people from all over the world to start moving to America. I guess people just know a good thing when they hear about it. Especially when they hear it has all this gold in it. It's probably not what Thomas Jefferson had in mind way back when he made the Louisiana Purchase, but I'm sure he was happy to see America growing into a place where so many people wanted to live. And just think: They hadn't even built Las Vegas or Disneyland yet!

Well, that's it for me. I'm Mel Roach, and, as usual, it's been a pleasure to help you learn about America's Funny But True History.

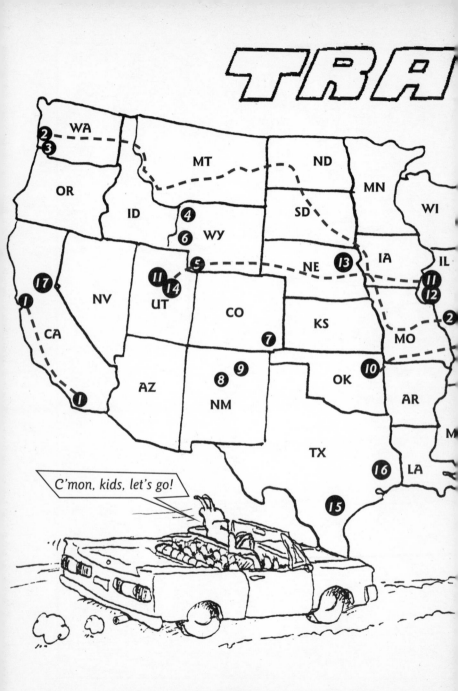

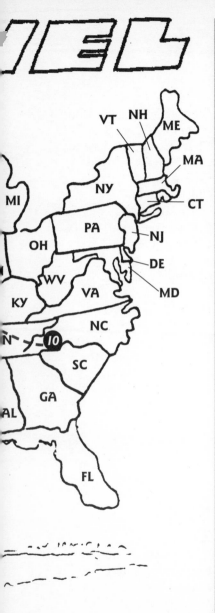

Index